WELFARE CHEESE
to
FINE CAVIAR

COMPANION GUIDE

THOMAS WIDEMAN MBA, PMP

Copyright © 2021 by Thomas Wideman
All rights reserved. This book or any portion thereof
may not be reproduced or used in any manner whatsoever
without the express written permission of the publisher
except for the use of brief quotations in a book review.

Cover design by Kristen Ingebretson
Interior layout and design by KUHN Design Group (kuhndesigngroup.com)
Developmental Editing by Rhonda Guyer (www.GuyerCopywriting.com)
Copyediting and Proofread by Lana Barnes

First Published in May 2021

ISBN: 978-1-7364630-3-1

Signs of Care Publishing
3595 Canton Road
Suite 312-149
Marietta, GA 30066

Printed in the United States of America on acid-free paper.

www.WelfareCheesetoFineCaviar.com

If you would like more information about authorizations,
speaking engagements and other products and services,
please visit our website or write publisher above.

Unless otherwise indicated, all Scripture quotations
are taking from King James Version (KJV)

I have tried to recreate events, locales and conversations from my memories of them. In order to maintain their anonymity in some instances I have changed the names of individuals and places, I may have changed some identifying characteristics and details such as physical properties, occupations and places of residence.

Although the author and publisher have made every effort to ensure that the information in this book was correct at press time, the author and publisher do not assume and hereby disclaim any liability to any party for any loss, damage, or disruption caused by errors or omissions, whether such errors or omissions result from negligence, accident, or any other cause.

Contents

How It Began	5
How to Use This Companion Guide	11
Poor No More	17
Peer Pressure and Race	35
The Thomas Special	53
The Death of a Role Model	69
I Am Never Getting Married	91
Control Your Response	109
The Payoff	127
Life is Short. Live It Well	141
Sharpen Your Focus	163
Loss	179
Fine Caviar	195
Final Thoughts	211
Professional Tidbits	213

How It Began

I never envisioned where the words would take me.

This is the poem that led to the writing of *Welfare Cheese to Fine Caviar*. It was my first attempt at opening my locked box of difficult experiences, some of which had been hidden away for decades. I lifted the lid only slightly. Over the years that followed, I could not escape my inner voice that whispered—then shouted— "It's time to take the lid off."

Father, Where Are You Taking Me?

Dear Father, where are You taking me?
You started me out in a single-parent home with
three younger brothers. Each of my brothers
had a different dad. Where was mine?
I was three years old when you let me see him last.
My brothers received gifts and money from their
dads. I received nothing, not even child support.
I later discovered that my dad was a murderer.
He killed his wife on the steps of Your House.
I appreciate You getting my dad away from my mom.
Father, where are You taking me?

You allowed my life to be a struggle from
the very beginning. As a child, other kids
picked on me because of my eyes.
They called me "cross-eyed," "Cyclops," "Dead Eye," and
other names that established a permanent emotional scar.
Even today, some people think that I am looking at
others when I am talking to them. But even with this
cosmetic flaw, You blessed me with Melanie, one of
the most beautiful, supportive wives in the world.
Father, where are You taking me?

You made me an outcast by terming me "gifted."
You took me out of classes with my friends and
placed me in ones where I did not fit in.
I did not have parents with professions.
My mom could not help me with my homework.
No one in my apartment complex could help me either.
In fact, my mom could not afford to send me on field
trips or pay for school lunch, much less college.
However, You always appeared through
someone or something…
Whether it was welfare, food stamps, free lunch,
student loans, scholarships, or generous people.
Father, where are You taking me?

You taught me about drugs early in my life.
You let me see them, touch them, and hold them.
You also showed me the effect of drugs.
My friends that were dealers had money, cars, jewelry, etc.
And when I considered giving up and becoming
a dealer, You introduced the real impact
of drugs when it mattered the most.
And oh, how I remember watching my grandmother,
one of the strongest women on this earth, cry for
her son who would break into the house, steal
things, and then run off into the night.
And when I thought that was the end of the lesson…
My best friend, whom I claimed as my older
brother, lost his life at the hands of another
so-called friend of ours because of the stuff.
But You always gave me the strength
to avoid using or selling them.
Father, where are You taking me?

You placed me in positions where I was in the spotlight.
In elementary school, You allowed me to sing at the
World's Fair in New Orleans, win two school spelling bees,
and attend special weekly regional brainstorming classes.
In high school, You made me student body vice president,
the starting cornerback on the football team, and a
student liaison for the Parent Teacher Association.
In college, you allowed me to attend a semester
at North Carolina State University through the
National Student Exchange Program, work a
summer in Texas as an Inroads intern with Union
Carbide Corporation, and attend conferences
in Baltimore, Greensboro, and Anaheim.
Father, where are You taking me?

You placed dreams in my head at night of
being a leader, but you never told me of what,
where, and whom I was going to lead.
You place me in leadership positions often.
However, You never tell me why.
According to my old boss, I earn more money
than 80 percent of the population.
But You guided me to budget every penny
to pay off debt and live for the future.
Father, where are You taking me?

You have given me high expectations for
myself and for those close to me.
And everyone, except my grandmother, has let me down.
But I still love them all.
When my head is in the clouds,
You knock me down to earth quickly.
When my back is against the ground, You raise me slowly.
But You are always there.
Father, where are You taking me?

I know there are others like me out there.
And I want to help show them the way.
But You continuously tell me that I am not ready yet.
Father, where are You taking me?
Father, please answer my prayers, so that
I may live Your will to the utmost.

Amen.

How to Use This Companion Guide

There came a moment when I realized my future was up to me, but only if I made vastly different choices in the present.

I wish I could be with you in person right now. I wish I could hear your story firsthand. The only reason I shared my story in *Welfare Cheese to Fine Caviar* was because I had you in mind. For years, I've lived with the thought swirling around in my mind that sharing my story might make a difference in someone else's life.

I want my story to make a difference in your life.

Not because my story is unique. But because it isn't. Because I know there are countless individuals who need to know they're not alone—and there is a way forward in the middle of seemingly insurmountable obstacles.

I know there are others like me out there.
And I want to help show them the way.

I can't be with you in person, but I can be with you through this guide.

I'm assuming you've already read *Welfare Cheese to Fine Caviar* (or you're reading it now) and you've picked up this Companion Guide because you want to change your life. You dream about a bright future in which you're fulfilled and happy and accomplishing great things. You just need to know someone cares. You need to know someone who knows the pain and struggles you're dealing with is pulling for you. You need someone to believe in you and take you seriously. Someone to point the way.

May I be that one?

LET'S DO THIS TOGETHER

We'll spend as much time together in these pages as you're willing to invest. I'll ask some hard questions—some you may not want to answer. I'll push you to look inward, challenge you to take responsibility for your life, give you action steps, and cheer you on!

I'm asking three things of you:

- **Give this process the time it deserves.** This book will guide you into change that will profoundly and positively impact your future. A few minutes here and there won't do it. You *have* all the time you need to invest in this process, but you may be filling that time with activities that are not moving you toward a happy and fulfilling future. Give this the priority it deserves because you're investing in your life.

- **Commit to the brutal honesty that will lead to change.** We're going to take this seriously, so there's no place for sidestepping the truth. When you pick up this Companion Guide, there's no place for anything except absolute honesty. This can be hard when you're looking inward, but it's also when it's the most important.

- **Do the hard work that change requires.** This means think deeply—and write. As you and I meet in these pages, your hard work (thinking and writing) is your investment in the process. More than that, it's your investment in yourself, your dreams, and your future.

STRUCTURE AND PACE

There is no timeline for finishing this book. I've designed some structure for you and have included suggestions below, but go through the process at your own pace. A word of caution, however. Make the commitment to go through this Companion Guide steadily, regularly. Don't let the process stretch out too long or you'll lose momentum.

> Make up your mind and commit your energy to achieving a better life.

- The chapters in this Companion Guide correspond to the same-titled chapters in *Welfare Cheese to Fine Caviar*.

- The words you'll read are just what I'd say to you if we could meet face to face. Carefully "listen" to what I share, then respond through your writing.

- I suggest that you complete the main section of each chapter in one sitting. If you must break it up into two consecutive days, review the first day's material before you begin the second day.

- "Caviar Time" is meant to be used daily in private. I wrote these positive messages as powerful "self-talk" to encourage you and equip you for change. You need to talk to yourself out loud to reinforce what you are learning about yourself. You need to "hear" the truths that will carry you into the future you dream about. Don't skip Caviar Time!

- You'll have two days—"Reflection Day One" and "Reflection Day Two"—to dig deeper into the subject of each chapter.

Well, there you have it. You've got everything you need to start an amazing journey toward your dreams.

I deeply believe that where you start in life does not have to be where you end up. If you want to do better and decide to do better and go after that with everything that you have, you can make it.

I don't have all the answers, but I've been where you are. I've overcome seemingly insurmountable obstacles to live a fulfilled, happy, prosperous life achieving great things. So I know it's possible.

Every struggle I've ever faced will have been worth it if I can help you reach the future of your dreams. Please shorten your journey by learning from mine.

I'm with you in this!

Thomas Wideman

"Not everything that is faced can be changed, but nothing can be changed until it is faced."

-JAMES BALDWIN-

Poor No More

When your life is in a ditch, change your perspective.

This time is important. It's time for you to look at your life's circumstances and the people in your life. But most important, it's time to look inward. Remember, don't close this book when the writing gets hard.... Keep pushing. This can change your life.

> *I didn't pick fights and tried to get along with everyone, but things were completely different. You had to fight to survive.*

Have you ever been in a situation or a season of life when you felt like you were fighting to survive? What did you feel was at stake?

Was it a fight for your soul?

For your peace?

For your well-being?

Was it a fight for your future, for your dreams?

What was it like? What did you experience? What did you feel?

Now, here's a more important question: *Are you there now?* Do you feel like you're fighting to survive? What do you feel is at stake? Are you fighting for your soul?

For your peace?

For your well-being?

Are you fighting for your future, for your dreams?

What is it like *now*? What are you experiencing? What do you feel?

Are you satisfied where you are?

What do you want to change?

> When your life is in a ditch, change your perspective.

In the chapter "Poor No More," I share my "in the ditch" moment. Have you had your "in the ditch" moment? It's the moment when circumstances or people are pounding you like you don't matter, like you're no one of consequence. The moment when you are confronted with where you are in life and you decide enough is enough.

What happened "in the ditch"?

_____

_____

_____

_____

_____

_____

_____

There is power in your "in the ditch" moment, but only if you let it open your eyes and propel you forward. And only if you're brave enough to be honest with yourself.

> But in that moment, I made up my mind to create a new life for myself.

Don't waste your "in the ditch" moment. Make it *that* moment. *That* moment when, like me, you make up your mind to create a new life for yourself.

First, change your mind. Then, change your life. How do you do that?

Keep reading.

Your "in the ditch" moment will propel you forward if you

- identify the real fight,
- take inventory,
- set your resolve, and
- do something.

Identify the real fight. Is the real fight with your circumstances? Is it with the people around you? Or is it with yourself—your beliefs about yourself, your expectations of yourself, your habits, your fears?

Take inventory. What gifts, natural talents, and skills do you possess?

Are you cultivating your gifts? Are you developing your natural talents? Are you sharpening your skills?

If you answered "no," why are you ignoring them?

Set your resolve. What has to change for your life to change? Recognize what is within your power to change—and determine to change it! The most important change will be the change in yourself.

Do something. This process will get you nowhere if you don't *do* something. What can you identify right now that you know you need to *start* doing? Or *stop* doing? What's on your mind?

> I would have to live up to my ability. I could no longer do the minimum, if I wanted to be free.

CAVIAR TIME

Go to the bathroom, bedroom, or any private room that has a mirror. Close and lock the door. Stare at yourself in the mirror. Repeat these words:

"God created me for a reason, and this is not it. My future must be better than where I am now. I commit today to first believe in my abilities to change my life to what I desire. Though I may not be that religious, I believe that God will guide me by speaking to me through my conscience, through the advice received from positive people, or by some other means. This can help to expand my knowledge, my network, and my experiences, which will seem uncomfortable at times.

"I am intelligent. Being smart does not mean that I have all the answers. It means that I realize what I know and that I need to seek answers to what I do not know.

"I am handsome/beautiful. The name-calling and rejections do not phase me. They are missing out on sharing this great gift that I possess. After I achieve my goals, they will want me more than I want them. If they do not, then there will be hundreds, maybe thousands, of others who will.

"God gave me gifts that I will discover and develop. I will achieve my goals or die trying. Every failure will only strengthen my resolve. Thomas Edison failed one thousand times before inventing the light bulb. I have the same or greater potential in me.

"Although society seems to hate or ignore me right now, my impact will be huge and beneficial for it. I am somebody with *great* potential!"

Reflection *Day One*

I am incredibly proud of you. You're investing time in the process of changing your life. You're honest about your situation and about yourself. You're doing the hard work—thinking deeply and writing.

This is how change happens!

Do you feel like you're fighting to survive in this season of your life? Go back and read what you wrote.

Now go back and read what you wrote about your "in the ditch" moment.

What three words describe the emotions you have as you reflect on what you've written?

Here's what I want you to do. Recognize the emotions—don't deny them—but turn them into fuel for change. Do not allow them to be in control of you. Feeding these negative emotions by dwelling on them only makes them stronger. Letting them go unchecked will defeat you and keep you from moving forward.

Feed your anger and your anger will grow.

Feed your hopelessness and your hopelessness will grow.

Feed your fear and your fear will grow.

Finish these statements with the emotions you identified.

If I feed my _____, my _____ will grow.

If I feed my _____, my _____ will grow.

If I feed my _____, my _____ will grow.

Think about this statement, then write it if you mean it: I am not willing to allow my negative emotions to keep me from moving forward.

_____

_____

> First, change your mind. Then, change your life.

Here are some keys to changing your mind about your negative emotions.

Be brutally honest. Name your negative emotions and be honest about how much they fuel the way you see your life and other people.

Examine the root. There's a reason these emotions overwhelm you. Examine what's at the root so you can understand yourself better—but don't dwell on the negative experiences at the root.

Tell yourself the truth. Negative emotions will sabotage your success. Use statements like these to speak the truth to yourself:

- Anger is not the path to my future. It will blind me to the good in people and to opportunities. Instead, I will choose action.

- Hopelessness is not the path to my future. I have hope because I have a bright mind and abilities, and *there is a way forward* to the happy, peaceful, and fulfilling life I desire. I understand that the choices for my future are mine.

- Fear is not the path to my future. I have the ability within me to be bold and make the decisions that will change me—and my life.

What truth do you need to tell yourself right now?

Today, I'll leave you with this:

Instead of looking backward, look forward with hope and anticipation because you've begun a journey that will take you to a future of fulfillment and achievement.

Instead of allowing negative emotions to overwhelm you, make them fuel for your resolve.

Instead of dwelling on the negative experiences of your life, focus on the possibilities for your future.

Your potential is greater than anything negative that has happened to you.

The future you dream of is ahead of you—and you walk forward by taking action. Take the next step.

Until next time,
Thomas

Reflection *Day Two*

Today, I want you to think about your gifts, natural talents, and skills. They are part of who you are. Recognizing, valuing, and developing them is key to your future.

This is how change happens!

Remember the "take inventory" section earlier in this chapter? Settle in and take a few minutes to review what you wrote.

Today, I want you to think a little more deeply.

What are your gifts? These are instinctive qualities. For instance, do you seem to know just how to encourage people? Do you have an instinctive ability to bring organization to situations?

Write about your gifts. Give me an example or two of how you use them.

This world needs you!

What are your natural talents? These are abilities that come easily to you. What things do you just "get" without having to be taught? For instance, are you a "natural" when it comes to math? Do you have a natural talent for problem-solving, piano, writing?

Write about your natural talents. Give me an example or two of how you use them.

What are your skills? These are abilities that you've learned, like photo editing, baking, or computer programming.

Write about your skills. Give me an example or two of how you use them.

> *Shorten your journey by learning from mine.*

Please listen to me, because I'm sharing something you can't ignore if you want to change your life.

Your gifts are meant to be cultivated.
Your natural talents are meant to be developed.
Your skills are meant to be sharpened.

But it will not happen automatically. You have to *do something*. Here are some ideas.

- Do you have a gift for compassion? You can cultivate it through visiting the elderly and helping them with chores.

- Do you have a natural talent for drawing? You can develop it by taking a free course on YouTube.

- Have you acquired baking skills? You can sharpen them by talking to your favorite cooks and asking for their best secrets.

Spend some time thinking deeply about your gifts, natural talents, and skills—then write.

I can cultivate my gift for _____ by

I can develop my natural talent for _____ by

_____
_____
_____
_____

I can sharpen my skill of _____ by

_____
_____
_____
_____
_____

If you competed the questions above, you have an action plan. Over the next week, do something to begin cultivating your gifts, developing your talents, and sharpening your skills.

I'm proud of you for investing in our time together in these pages, because that means you're investing in yourself and your future. I'm proud of you for looking inward and resolving to take action.

Keep it up! Until next time,
Thomas

"Progress is impossible without change, and those who cannot change their minds cannot change anything."

-GEORGE BERNARD SHAW-

Peer Pressure and Race

An open mind beats a closed fist any day.

This time is important. It's time for you to look at the way you view other people, to examine the stereotypes you've bought into and the false assumptions you hold. Remember, don't close this book when the writing gets hard.... Keep pushing. This can change your life.

> *First, change your mind. Then, change your life.*

You've already read this more than once:

"First, change your mind. Then, change your life."

You're going to read it again and again. By the time we finish our journey through these pages, I want you to have no doubt about the power of your mind and the impact your thoughts have on your life and your relationships.

I want you to understand the importance of valuing people, and I want you to understand that the way you treat them starts in your mind. In other words, your thoughts about others dictate how you treat them.

Before we go further, take a moment to write your definition of the two words below.

Stereotype:

Assumption:

Were your definitions something like these I gleaned from a Google search?

Stereotype: a preconceived idea that is used to describe a type of person or group of people.[1]

---

1. *Cambridge Dictionary*, s.v. "stereotype (*n.*)," accessed February 15, 2021, https://dictionary.cambridge.org/us/dictionary/english/stereotype; *Vocabulary.com*, s.v., "stereotype (*n.*)," accessed February 15, 2021, https://www.vocabulary.com/dictionary/stereotype.

Assumption: something that you accept as true without question or proof, something taken as being true or factual and used as a starting point for a course of action or reasoning.[1]

Stereotypes and assumptions go hand in hand. Read this description:

> *His dark gray suit was tailored to highlight his physique. Steely-eyed, he pushed briskly through the revolving door of the downtown high-rise and, with the help of his Bluetooth earpiece, continued negotiating with his client. He was a stereotype of the latest flood of hotshot thirtysomething stockbrokers to move into the city.*

Let's say you observed this scene firsthand. What are your assumptions about this man?

Here's another description:

> *She was obviously frazzled and close to her wits' end. Both of the children she had in tow, the girl on her hip and the boy she pulled along by his wrist, were under the age of three. The trio was disheveled and wearing clothes in desperate need of laundering. Both children were crying—the kind of cry that comes when a child is tired and fighting sleep. As she clumsily*

---

1. *Cambridge Dictionary*, s.v. "assumption (*n.*)," accessed February 15, 2021, https://dictionary.cambridge.org/us/dictionary/english/assumption.; *Merriam-Webster*, s.v. "assumption (*n.*)," accessed February 15, 2021, https://www.merriam-webster.com/thesaurus/assumption.

strapped them into the hand-me-down safety seats in the back of her faded Oldsmobile, the young woman began to cry too. "Well," my aunt said in a superior tone as we crossed the parking lot near the faded Oldsmobile, "there's the stereotype of the girls from McCandry County."

Let's say you observed this scene firsthand. What are your assumptions about the young woman with the crying children?

_____

_____

_____

_____

_____

_____

The problem with a stereotype is that it is an overgeneralized belief about a particular group of people that causes us to have expectations about *every person* in that group.[1] Unfortunately, a stereotype is most commonly negative—a misinformed, preconceived notion that is based on prejudice.

A negative stereotype breeds false assumptions. Those false assumptions dictate how we treat people, what we expect of them. We make determinations about people in advance. We believe something that we don't examine, and we treat people according to mistaken beliefs, not according to what is true of them.

---

1. Dr. Saul McLeod, "Stereotypes," SimplyPsychology, updated 2017, https://www.simplypsychology.org/katz-braly.html.

> *But Pelham Road opened my eyes to other possibilities. Maybe people of diverse backgrounds do want you to succeed.*

In the chapter "Peer Pressure and Race," I share the story of my trip to sing at the 1984 World's Fair in New Orleans with the Pelham Road Elementary School All-Star Chorus. I rode a bus across town to attend Pelham, a well-resourced school where the rich white people sent their kids. Even at that young age, I had false assumptions:

- "White people don't want you to succeed."
- "People like me will always be poor."

I was a talented singer and loved being part of the chorus, but there was no way we could afford the trip to New Orleans. Then the unexpected happened. One of those rich white people who I was sure cared nothing for me paid all my expenses for the trip. My assumptions were wrong, and I had the amazing opportunity to sing at the World's Fair.

The quality of your life is directly related to the quality of your relationships.

IDENTIFY THE REAL FIGHT.

Write what you've come to understand about why you treat people the way you do.

TAKE INVENTORY.

I want you to examine your beliefs. That's how change starts.

What are the negative stereotypes you've bought into?

What are the false assumptions you have about particular groups of people?

> "Treat everyone with respect and love because you don't know what angels God will send to assist you." —Grandma

Here's the toughest question of all. How does your behavior toward certain groups of people reflect your false assumptions about them?

SET YOUR RESOLVE.

Make the decision to reject negative stereotypes and false assumptions. Read these statements out loud.

"I will reject negative stereotypes and false assumptions because I value people."

"I will reject negative stereotypes and false assumptions because I want to be a positive force in people's lives."

"I will reject negative stereotypes and false assumptions because they close doors that should be open."

"I will reject negative stereotypes and false assumptions because they keep me from relationships that could enrich my life."

"I will reject negative stereotypes and false assumptions because they keep me from growing to my greatest potential."

"I will reject negative stereotypes and false assumptions because they keep me from learning a different perspective that will enlarge my understanding."

Add your own.

"I will reject negative stereotypes and false assumptions because

_____."

"I will reject negative stereotypes and false assumptions because

_____."

DO SOMETHING.

All change requires you to be intentional. What can you do (or stop doing) as of now to reject negative stereotypes and false assumptions? I'll give you a few ideas.

- Have a response ready when someone speaks negatively about a group of people. "Hey, we don't know them. Why would we talk about people we don't even know?" Or "I'm learning that negative stereotypes only make things worse between people. I don't want to hear those things anymore."

- Get to know people who are different from me. (Does a specific person come to mind, someone you've shied away from?)

- Read about people who are different from me.

- Stop forming opinions about a whole group of people because of a bad experience with one person.

-

-

-

-

When we are receptive and open to "other people," it can expand our dreams, broaden our possibilities, increase our knowledge, and enlarge our capacity to succeed and positively impact our world.

One more thing before you go, read this statement out loud:

"This is how I change the world one person at a time. I don't interact according to negative stereotypes and false assumptions."

Now write it here. Or better yet, write in on an index card and tape it to your mirror.

> *To achieve my goals, I have to find a diverse group of people to help me.*

CAVIAR TIME

Go to the bathroom, bedroom, or any private room that has a mirror. Close and lock the door. Stare at yourself in the mirror. Repeat these words:

"God has granted me with the knowledge, desire, and characteristics that I need to be successful. The rest is up to me. I can do this.

"To achieve my goals, I have to find a diverse group of people to help me. I realize that I must give in order to receive. Without the expectation of compensation, I will give them my attention, my sweat, my respect, and my time in return for knowledge and opportunity. I will smile, even when their words may hurt me, and resist the urge to react with emotion. No person's words have the power to ruin me unless I allow them. I will not always assume that their words are intended to harm me. Instead, I will take stock of the little nuggets of wisdom and education buried in the rough. I will smile and treat everyone with respect. I will greet my elders with sir, ma'am, mister, or missus, unless instructed otherwise.

"God will place people in my life to help me and others to test my resolve. I need them both. I got this!"

Reflection *Day One*

I hope you're proud of yourself. I'm sure proud of you! You are willing to do the hard work for a future you can be excited about. You're willing to look inside yourself and examine your beliefs about people and the way you treat them. You're willing to confront negative stereotypes and false assumptions head-on so they lose their power over your life.

This is how change happens!

I want you to understand how critical it is for you to take personal responsibility for your future. That means taking responsibility for your thoughts and actions. As I was growing up, I didn't see this modeled very often. Do you know someone who models this for you? Who is it, and how do you see them taking responsibility for their thoughts and actions?

Confronting stereotypes and assumptions is one way to take responsibility for your future. Another way is to refuse to play the blame game. In the chapter "Peer Pressure and Race," I share this:

> *I was surrounded by people who blamed the government, rich white people, and sometimes even God for their failures. I also noticed that these people had limited dreams.*

Blaming others for your failures will limit your dreams. Blaming others means you see your success or failure as someone else's responsibility. When you play the blame game, you, in effect, surrender your future to someone else. You essentially take yourself off the hook and live off excuses.

Are you blaming anyone else for your failures? Are you depending on someone else to bring you success? Take a moment to look inward, and then write what comes to mind.

Another way to take responsibility for your future is to reject peer pressure. Remember the story I share in "Peer Pressure and Race" about my friends pressuring me to fight the heavyset white guy walking to the store with his little brother? One of my friends called the guy "Fatso" and another friend falsely accused the guy of using the N-word. With the pressure on me, I decided to save face by giving the guy a little push. Then he pulled out a knife and lunged at me.

None of my options were very good at that moment, but I mustered up the courage to stand up to the peer pressure instead of pursuing a fight. I decided to treat the guy as he deserved instead of treating him the way my friends wanted me to. The guy was no different from me. He was walking his little brother to the store. The same store we were walking to.

> *"God has a way of dealing with ugly."* —Grandma

Are your friends influencing you to do something you know is not right? Are they pressuring you to make a decision that you know is not in your best interest?

How can you stand up to the pressure and do the right thing?

Until next time,
Thomas

Reflection *Day Two*

Today, I want you to think more about your gifts, natural talents, and skills. Remember, they are part of who you are. Recognizing, valuing, and developing them is key to your future.

This is how change happens!

> *Someone sponsored my entire trip... and I didn't take it for granted... I gave the best performance my little lungs could provide.*

In "Peer Pressure and Race," I share about the unexpected gift of having my expenses paid so I could travel to the 1984 World's Fair in New Orleans with the Pelham Road Elementary School All-Star Chorus. I learned important lessons from that experience that I want to share with you.

False assumptions are just that. False. I believed the rich white parents whose kids went to Pelham School didn't care a thing about a poor kid like me. I thought I was invisible to them, but I wasn't. They saw me. And one of them paid all my expenses so I could travel to New Orleans and sing with the chorus.

Be grateful for your natural talents. Your talents are God-given and are part of who you are. Don't hide them—they're meant to be used! Value them and develop them.

Be grateful for the people who encourage you and help you. Encouragement and help may come from unexpected places. Don't ever take them for granted, and be intentional in expressing your gratitude to those who invest in your life.

> *God will place people in my life to help me and others to test my resolve. I need them both.*

I want you to go back to "Poor No More," and review what you wrote for Reflection Day Two—**but first, read the rest of this page for instructions.**

Thoughtfully review what you wrote in the last chapter about your gifts, natural talents, and skills. Write any other thoughts, questions, or insights that come to mind. Record other examples of how you're using your gifts, talents, and skills.

Next, review the section where you find the statements below. (You formed your action plan by working through this section.) After you review it, come back here.

Your gifts are meant to be cultivated.

Your natural talents are meant to be developed.

Your skills are meant to be sharpened.

In "Poor No More" Reflection Day Two, I asked you to do something over the following week to begin cultivating your gifts, developing your talents, and sharpening your skills. How are you doing with that? Honestly assess the steps you've taken. If you haven't taken any action, why?

If you're doing well with this, I hope you're excited about investing in yourself! If you haven't taken any action, don't beat yourself up, but ask yourself this question: What will it take for me to invest in my future by cultivating my gifts, developing my natural talents, and sharpening my skills?

You've got this! Until next time,
Thomas

"If we magnified blessings as much as we magnify disappointments, we would all be much happier."

-JOHN WOODEN-

The Thomas Special

Ill intent and revenge lead to a killer headache.

This time is important. It's time for you to look at the importance of staying in control and letting go of revenge. Remember, don't close this book when the writing gets hard.…Keep pushing. This can change your life.

> *First, change your mind. Then, change your life.*

In *Welfare Cheese to Fine Caviar*, I share openly about my upbringing. I invite you into the dysfunction, disappointment, and difficulty of life as I knew it.

> *One day I got in trouble with my stepdad for whatever reason, but I didn't think I deserved it. I was only in elementary school, but I often felt my punishments were undeserving; I really had a chip on my shoulder back then. I'm the oldest of four boys, but all of us have different fathers. Mine was the only one who was never around. The last time I saw him, I was three years old.*

> *Even though I was a kid, I was pretty much the man of the house. At least that's what I felt. As the oldest boy, I had always been in charge of my brothers. Men would come and go, but whenever they were there, they would take over as man of the house (according to them, at least). If you asked me, it was my domain, and I didn't appreciate anyone coming in to claim my territory. That's where things stood with my stepdad. He pulled rank, and I was in trouble.*
>
> *He drank alcohol and enjoyed mixing some cocktails. He'd pour them in plastic soda bottles and drink them whenever he was in the mood. That day, I decided to mix a Thomas Special. "I'll show him who's the man in this house," I thought.*[1]

If you remember the story, it didn't end so well for me.

The entire revenge-laden sixteen ounces of that nasty alcoholic concoction I intended for my stepdad was forced on me. Every drop. As dangerous as my mom and stepdad's choice of punishment was, I survived. But I got drunk. Sloppy drunk.

A young boy in elementary school should never have to learn the lesson I did, but I learned it well. As drunk as I was, I remember the feeling of being completely out of control—my mind, body, and emotions under the influence of a substance stronger than I was. I decided then and there not to drink alcohol ever again, and I've been alcohol free most of my entire life.

> If I planned to live the life I wanted, I needed to remain focused and on track. The only way to stay focused was to stay in control. So I did.

---

1. Wideman, Thomas. *Welfare Cheese to Fine Caviar: How to Achieve Your Dreams Despite Your Upbringing.* Marietta: Signs of Care Publishing, 2021, 53–54.

IDENTIFY THE REAL FIGHT.

I came to understand that the real fight was not against my stepdad, but was against my angry perception of my life. The real fight was conquering my desire for revenge and defending myself against anything that would cause me to lose control of my mind, body, or emotions.

What is your real fight?

TAKE INVENTORY.

As a young boy, I knew I never wanted to be completely out of control again. The other lessons of that incident developed more slowly as I matured. Have you learned the lessons I've outlined below?

A tough life doesn't give me permission to take revenge. I wanted to take revenge on my stepdad because he disciplined me without having the authority (in my mind) to do so.

Have you ever wanted to take revenge on someone? Who was it—and why?

Revenge doesn't put me in control. I felt in control as I plotted revenge on my stepdad, but I wasn't. Revenge twisted my thinking and gave me the illusion of power.

Did you take revenge on that person you wrote about above? What happened? How did you feel?

Alcohol and drugs are not the only things that can cause me to forfeit control. I may not turn to alcohol or drugs, but there are plenty of other ways I can escape my troubles and become detached from reality. Even "innocent" distractions when taken to the extreme can be as debilitating as substance abuse. Addiction to social media, gaming, thrill-seeking, and spending are examples of abuses that wreak havoc on individuals and families. What other addictions can you name?

Have you seen or experienced the devastation addiction causes?

What do you turn to for distraction when things get tough? Whatever activity it is, do you approach it in a healthy way? Does it cause you to detach from reality?

> You can choose the action, but you can't always control the outcome, especially when you are acting out of revenge.

When I allow myself to lose control of my mind, body, and emotions, I am gambling with my future. I risk relationships, opportunities, good outcomes, financial stability, and more. I risk causing harm or irreversible consequences to myself or someone else. Let's be real—I risk my life or someone else's.

Do you allow yourself to lose control of your mind, body, and emotions because of drugs or alcohol? Do you abuse other activities as a way to escape reality?

SET YOUR RESOLVE.

Make the decision to always stay in control of your mind, body, and emotions, never giving them over to any substance or unhealthy influence.

Write about your resolve in your own words. Why are you making this decision?

READ THIS IMPORTANT NOTE:

Please don't treat this subject lightly. If you have a problem with substance abuse or any type of addiction, you need help to overcome it. I am not a healthcare professional, and I'm not qualified to help you overcome substance abuse.

I do know that you need to make winning over your addiction your number one priority right now. Never be ashamed of what you need. Confide in a trusted family member or friend and get help.

You can start by calling the SAMHSA (Substance Abuse and Mental Health Services Administration) National Helpline at 1-800-662-4357. Right now.

DO SOMETHING.

All change requires you to be intentional. Be your own compassionate friend and use this space to write to yourself about substance abuse. What do you want to say?

THIS NEEDS REPEATING:

Please don't treat this subject lightly. If you have a problem with substance abuse or any type of addiction, you need help to overcome it. I am not a healthcare professional, and I'm not qualified to help you overcome substance abuse.

I do know that you need to make winning over your addiction your number one priority right now. Never be ashamed of what you need. Confide in a trusted family member or friend and get help.

You can start by calling the SAMHSA (Substance Abuse and Mental Health Services Administration) National Helpline at 1-800-662-4357. Right now.

Do not act on revenge. No one ever wins.

CAVIAR TIME

Go back to your private space used in the previous chapter or find a new one. Close and lock the door. Stare at yourself in the mirror. Repeat these words:

"I am intelligent, handsome/beautiful, and loved. I can feel the change that God is making in me. Although I am not experiencing the fruits of my labor, I can picture myself in possession of my goals.

"I have met a few people who are helping me. Some don't know that they are doing so. I have met others who are testing my resolve. They continue to mistreat, ignore, or disrespect me. I pay no attention to them and use my anger to push me even harder. I am going to show them. I admit that the first set of insults cut me deep emotionally. However, I have grown thicker skin that is getting harder each day. I will not seek revenge. Instead, I will smile and treat them nicely as I silently recite, 'God, forgive them for they know not what they do.' I forgive them. To achieve my objectives, I always need complete focus. One mistake for me could cost me my goals, my freedom, or my life. Therefore, I will not use drugs, drink alcohol, or cede control of my thoughts or actions to any person, group, or organization unless it is helping me meet my objective. Even then, I will question that occurrence to ensure that I am on the right path, especially to consider God speaking to me through my conscience.

"In closing, I know this is hard. I see my friends playing and having fun while I study. I do spend some time with them, but I am on a different path. One that will greatly benefit my loved ones and me. I feel the changes stirring in me!"

Reflection *Day One*

You are doing a great job! You're considering important issues that directly impact your life now and in the future. You're willing to confront the hard stuff.

Keep doing the hard work and you will have every reason to be excited about your future.

This is how change happens!

> *The seed for your future is in your mind right now.*

I want you to understand that what you allow to influence you *will* impact your life and your future. And you can choose what you allow to influence you.

The seed for your future is in your mind right now. You possess God-given gifts right now. You display natural talents right now. You have used your brain and your determination to acquire skills that are useful right now.

Please listen carefully. You are allowing influences into your life *right now* that are affecting your growth, your vision, your perspective, your desires, and ultimately, your future.

Messages are coming at you from just about everywhere. Celebrities, music, advertising, social media, TV, movies, books, magazines, politicians, activists, friends, family…The list is nearly unending. They're all competing for your attention. They all want to be a major influence in your life. They want you to look, think, and act like they say. They want you to want what they want. They want you to believe their message is the most important.

I've heard it said—and it's true—if you don't have a plan for your life, you'll just live out someone else's plan for your life. Take a moment to think about that.

> *If you watch or listen to anything long enough, you start to believe that those things are true.*

I want you to settle in for some self-evaluation about the messages you take in every day. Think deeply about the questions below and then spend some time writing in response.

- To what and to whom do you give most of your attention?

- How is most of your time spent?

- Who is influencing you? Think beyond family, friends, coworkers, teachers.

- How many hours a week are you reading and what are you reading?

- How many hours a week are you devoting to entertainment? What kind of entertainment? (FYI: social media is entertainment.)

- What messages do you hear most often?

- Given all the influences you have in your life, what or who is actually the strongest influence?

Until next time,
Thomas

Reflection *Day Two*

Today, we're going to spend time again focusing on your gifts, natural talents, and skills. I'm going to keep reminding you that they are part of who you are.

This is how change happens!

Recognizing, valuing, and developing your gifts, natural talents, and skills is key to your future, so we're going back to "Poor No More" Reflection Day Two.

First, read this page all the way through for instructions.

Go to "Poor No More" and review what you wrote for Reflection Day Two.

Thoughtfully consider how you described your gifts, natural talents, and skills. Write any other thoughts, questions, or insights that come to mind. Record other examples of how you're using your gifts, talents, and skills.

Next, review the action plan you formed in the section where you find the statements below. Then, come back to this page.

Your gifts are meant to be cultivated.

Your natural talents are meant to be developed.

Your skills are meant to be sharpened.

How are you doing with your action plan? Honestly assess the steps you've taken. If you haven't taken any action, why?

If you're doing well with this, I hope you're thoroughly enjoying investing in yourself! It will pay off.

If you haven't taken any action, don't beat yourself up, but ask yourself this question again: What will it take for me to invest in my future and start cultivating my gifts, developing my natural talents, and sharpening my skills? What's your answer?

Now, do one more thing. Share with a trusted family member or friend the journey that you're on to change your life. Talk with them about your desire to invest in your future. Talk with them about your gifts and talents and skills. Be honest about the difficulty you're having committing to action steps. Ask them for their support and ask them two questions:

1. Because you know me well and I trust you, will you share with me any insight you have as to why committing to action steps may be hard for me?

2. Will you help me develop a plan to carve out the time and place to develop my gifts and talents and skills?

Record it all here.

You've got this! Until next time,
Thomas

"The artist is nothing without the gift, but the gift is nothing without work."

-ÉMILE ZOLA-

The Death of a Role Model

Holding a drug addict's money for safekeeping can be bad for your health.

This time is important. We're going to talk about an uncomfortable subject. What do you do if someone close to you is addicted to drugs or alcohol? If you don't think this chapter applies to you, please keep reading. I promise, you need this chapter. Remember, don't close this book when the writing gets hard....Keep pushing. This can change your life.

> *First, change your mind. Then, change your life.*

Substance abuse is not confined to a gender, an age bracket, an education level, a socioeconomic level, or a neighborhood. You may have someone close to you now who is addicted to alcohol or drugs.

Do you?

Your life may already be affected by someone else's addiction. Is it?

If not now, the likelihood is high that in the future you will be impacted by someone else's substance abuse. Take a look at the statistics below.

- In 2017, an estimated 20.7 million people age 12 and older battled a substance use disorder. Only 4 million people received treatment.[1]
- About 38% of adults in 2017 battled an illicit drug use disorder.[2]
- That same year, 1 out of every 8 adults struggled with both alcohol and drug use disorders simultaneously.[3]
- Over half of all American adults have a family history of problem drinking or alcohol addiction.[4]
- 40% of all hospital beds in the United States are used to treat conditions related to alcohol consumption.[5]
- Drug abuse and addiction cost American society more than $740 billion annually in lost workplace productivity, healthcare expenses, and crime-related costs.[6]
- More than 10% of U.S. children live with a parent with alcohol problems.[7]

---

1. Substance Abuse and Mental Health Services Administration, *Key Substance Use and Mental Health Indicators in the United States: Results from the 2017 National Survey on Drug Use and Health*, September 7, 2018, https://www.samhsa.gov/data/sites/default/files/cbhsq-reports/NSDUHDetailedTabs2017/NSDUHDetailedTabs2017.pdf.
2. Ibid.
3. Ibid.
4. Vertava Health, *Alcohol Abuse Statistics*, August 16, 2019, https://vertavahealth.com/blog/alcohol-abuse-statistics/.
5. Northstar Transitions, Alcohol Use Disorder Treatment Awareness, April 24, 2019, https://www.northstartransitions.com/post/alcohol-use-disorder-treatment-awareness#:~:text=NCADD%20reports%20that%2040%20percent,use%20disorder%20develops%20over%20decades.
6. National Institute on Drug Abuse, *Trends & Statistics*, accessed February 18, 2021, https://www.drugabuse.gov/drug-topics/trends-statistics.
7. National Institute on Alcohol Abuse and Alcoholism, *Alcohol Facts and Statistics*, accessed February 18, 2021, https://www.niaaa.nih.gov/publications/brochures-and-fact-sheets/alcohol-facts-and-statistics

- The highest at-risk population for heroin addiction is non-Hispanic white males between the ages of 18 and 25 who live in large cities.[1]
- Whites had a 7.7% rate of substance abuse in 2017.[2]
- About 6.8% percent of African Americans struggled with substance use disorders, while the percentage of Hispanics or Latinos who suffered from substance use disorders was 6.6%.[3]

Do any of these statistics surprise you? If so, what?

As you reviewed the statistics, did you discover that some of your assumptions about people with substance abuse are false? What are they?

---

1. Centers for Disease Control and Prevention, *Today's Heroin Epidemic*, July 7, 2015, https://www.cdc.gov/vitalsigns/heroin/index.html
2. Substance Abuse and Mental Health Services Administration, *Key Substance Use and Mental Health Indicators in the United States: Results from the 2017 National Survey on Drug Use and Health*, September 7, 2018, https://www.samhsa.gov/data/sites/default/files/cbhsq-reports/NSDUHDetailedTabs2017/NSDUHDetailedTabs2017.pdf.
3. Ibid.

> *I was fifteen years old and the man of the house for most of my life, so I did what I was used to doing. I put myself in charge.*

There was a time when I didn't want anyone to know about the addiction in my family. But just like I learned that an addiction kept secret has no chance of losing its power, I've learned that a story kept secret has no chance of *offering* its power. My story is unique in its details, but not in its theme. There is a way forward when someone you love is addicted, but you won't believe it unless you hear someone else's story.

For a long time, my family was "all in," doing whatever we thought was necessary to help Uncle Rico get clean. We believed "we" could overcome his addiction. Finally, after seemingly unending cycles of collective hope and excruciating disappointment, everyone in our family was exhausted and gave up. Everyone, that is, except me. I still held on to the belief that I could do the work for Uncle Rico.

I was wrong.

What about you? Are you taking the responsibility for someone else's recovery on your shoulders? Are you trying to do the work for them? What are you doing to "help" the situation? Are you trying to shield them from the consequences of their behavior? Trying to protect other people you love from the consequences?

Here's a dose of brutal honesty: what you consider "help" may actually be enabling your loved one to continue in their addiction.

The harrowing night that Uncle Rico came after the money he'd given me for safekeeping brought me face-to-face with a drug-crazed zombie I barely recognized as my uncle. Grandma saw him kick down the door of my bedroom and scream at me to hand over the child-support money. "Don't let me come back and get it!" he'd demanded only hours before. Grandma understood something I did not. The drugs were calling the shots now for Uncle Rico. She courageously took charge to get me out of danger. "Pukey, give him that money right now!"

With that incident, I finally began to see my uncle's addiction for what it was: an illness that no amount of effort on my part could make go away. The addiction was the killer of dreams. It was depleting everyone around it. No matter how much we pleaded with my uncle, loved him, cheered him on, or willed him to change, we could not take a single step toward recovery for him.

Your loved one needs compassion and support, but they need compassion that is informed and support that is appropriate. Uninformed compassion is a deep and caring concern that lacks an understanding of the dynamics of addiction. It causes us to make excuses and see ourselves in an unrealistic role as a rescuer or fixer. Inappropriate support is "help" that actually enables addictive behavior. It causes us to shield our loved one from the consequences of their choices.

You must come to terms with the fact that the work of recovery cannot be done by you. You must educate yourself about addiction so that you can offer compassion and support that keeps your loved one's recovery as the goal but places the responsibility for it fully on their shoulders. The Substance Abuse and Mental Health Services Administration is a good place to start. Visit their website at www.samhsa.gov/families.

> "Pukey, give him that money right now." —Grandma

Are you coming to terms with who is responsible for your loved one's recovery? Every step of their recovery is theirs to take, *not yours*. If your loved one will not take those steps, it *does not* reflect an inadequacy or failure on your part.

What do you need to say to yourself right now?

_____

_____

_____

_____

_____

_____

One more thing I want you to understand. When it comes to interacting with a person who is addicted to drugs or alcohol, actions speak louder than words. No matter what they say, the truth will always be found in what they do. For instance, even though Uncle Rico said he wanted to get clean, he kept going back to the same people and places that fueled his addiction. No amount of words will accomplish what only action can.

> The uncle I loved was still there, but my role model was gone.

IDENTIFY THE REAL FIGHT.

The real fight is not against the person who is addicted, but against the addiction itself. As I had to admit of my uncle Rico, "the drugs call the shots."

Think about your loved one who is controlled by substance abuse.

Write their name here.

What are they addicted to?

What is the real fight?

TAKE INVENTORY.

Thinking again of your loved one, how do you see their addiction affecting their life?

How do you see your loved one's addiction affecting the people around them? How does it affect *you*?

Do you feel responsible for your loved one's recovery?

If you answered "yes," why do you feel that responsibility?

Have you talked with anyone about your loved one's addiction or are you trying to deal with it privately? Have you talked with a healthcare professional?

You can't save everyone when you are trying to save yourself.

SET YOUR RESOLVE.

Make these statements real for your situation, then say them out loud.

I am not responsible for _____'s recovery.

It is impossible for me to take steps for _____.

Every step in recovery from addiction must be taken by _____.

I will no longer think of myself as _____'s rescuer or fixer.

DO SOMETHING.

- Tell someone. Make sure it is someone wise and caring. You need support as you navigate your loved one's addiction. **You are not alone**, so do not allow yourself to feel as if you are. Any addiction kept hidden will always be in charge.

- Get professional help for yourself. You need more than family and good friends supporting you. You need help from a healthcare professional. Start by calling the SAMHSA (Substance Abuse and Mental Health Services Administration) National Helpline at 1-800-662-4357.

PLEASE READ THIS IMPORTANT MESSAGE:

I am not a healthcare professional, and I'm not qualified to help anyone overcome substance abuse. **I do know that if you have a loved one struggling with substance abuse, you are being affected by it and you need help in dealing with it. Make that a priority.** You can start by calling the SAMHSA (Substance Abuse and Mental Health Services Administration) National Helpline at 1-800-662-4357. Right now.

> He paused, then the words came out of his own mouth. "I'm on crack."

CAVIAR TIME

Go to your private space or find a new one. Close and lock the door. Stare at yourself in the mirror. Repeat these words:

"I can feel God working in my life. My attitude and perspective have changed. I accept my surroundings and struggles, because I know that it is temporary. I take pride in every good grade, promotion, or other achievement. I will not let any substance or person steer me away from my destiny.

"I love my family and friends dearly. I will teach them what I know, aid them in struggles not self-initiated, and celebrate their achievements. I will not allow their bad decisions to deter me from my goals. This will be one of the most difficult decisions of my life. I understand that I can do more for them once I achieve my goals than I can in my current state. If they love me as much I love them, then they will see it the same way I do.

"The path I have chosen is difficult. While my peers seem to enjoy life, I am constantly making difficult decisions and analyzing the results and effects on people. No one seems to understand or believe my vision or why I am constantly out of my comfort zone. However, I dream of me being in possession of my goals. I experience setbacks, but their impact gets weaker each time. I will do this!"

Reflection *Day One*

You are showing yourself to be brave. You are not avoiding the difficult issues, and I'm proud of you. You are learning how to care for yourself and the people you love while you keep moving toward your future. You'll never regret this season of challenge and growth, and down the road you'll understand more clearly how it was part of your journey to the future you desire.

This is how change happens!

> *Man, I want to grow up to be just like him.*

What is your definition of a role model?

Who is your role model? Perhaps you have more than one.

What qualities do you see in your role model(s) that you want to emulate?

Does your role model(s) possess negative qualities that you ignore?

What are those negative qualities?

Why do you think you ignore them?

Here's a word of caution. Negative qualities have negative consequences—for you and the people you care about. Do not excuse the negative qualities you discover in yourself because you see them in your role model.

> Love your family and understand that the best thing you could ever do for them is for YOU to achieve success.

Do you know that *you* are someone's role model? You are impacting someone's life right now more than you know. Someone is paying attention to you. Someone wants to be like you. Who's coming to mind?

_____

Think about a person you care about. It could be the person you just named or it could be a brother, sister, cousin, or friend. What qualities do you see in them? Write about them here as if you're talking to them.

_____, this is what I see in you.

_____

_____

_____

When you think about their future, what do you want for them? Think more deeply than a good job and money. Write about it here as if you're talking to them.

_____, this is what I hope for your future.

_____

_____

_____

_____

Chances are that the words you just wrote were kind and generous. I imagine you pointed out the special qualities you admire. I'm guessing you painted a picture of their future that would inspire them to develop their gifts and talents and skills.

I have a question for you now. Are you that kind and generous to yourself? What qualities do you see in yourself? What do you want for your future?

Take a few moments and write to yourself.

_____, this is what I see in you.

_____, this is what I hope for your future.

Now, read those notes to yourself out loud.

Until next time,
Thomas

"Be careful how you are talking to yourself because you are listening."

LISA M. HAYES

Reflection *Day Two*

Today, we're going to talk about your "trusted few," the several people in your life you can look to for support. You can't complete the journey into your future alone. There are people in your life who care deeply about you and who can offer you the kind of encouragement and support you need. Don't overlook them!

This is how change happens!

Who are your "trusted few"—the friends or family members with whom you can talk openly about your goals and dreams? Maybe there's only one. That's okay. Name them.

_____

_____

_____

Have you shared with them about your journey to invest in your future?

_____

Have you talked with them about your gifts and natural talents and skills?

_____

Have you described the changes you want to see in your life?

_____

What was their response? Did you sense genuine support? How did you feel afterward?

It's important to have a trusted few (or one) in your life to look to for support. What do you think you need from them? (I've started the list for you.)

- I need them to have my best interest at heart.
- I need them to be honest with me.
- I need them to be willing to tell me things I may not want to hear.
-
-
-
-
-

As you receive input from your trusted few, what do you think they need from you? (I've started the list for you.)

- They need me to listen without getting defensive.

- They need me to understand that I have blind spots, and they can often see what I can't.

- They need me to take them seriously.

-

-

-

-

-

If you couldn't name a trusted few (or one), here's what I want you to do over the next few days. Think about the people in your life—family, friends, neighbors, teachers, coworkers. Which of them could be your trusted few?

Talk with them about being one of your trusted few. Have that first conversation.

Tell them you're serious about making decisions that will ensure the future of your dreams. Thank them for being willing to encourage you and give you input.

> God gave me gifts that I will discover and develop.

If you were able to name your trusted few, here's what I want you to do over the next few days. If you haven't already done so, talk with them about this journey you are on. (That may have been your assignment as part of "The Thomas Special" Reflection Day Two.) Tell them you're serious about making decisions that will ensure the future of your dreams. Thank them for being willing to encourage you and give you input.

Now, one more thing. On Reflection Day One of this chapter, you wrote a message to someone you care about. You described to them the qualities you see in them and the hopes you have for their future. So, do it for real. Write a note, send an email or a text, make a quick call.... Just tell that someone what you wrote. Be one of *their* trusted few.

You've got this! Until next time,
Thomas

"Talent is like electricity. We don't understand electricity. We use it"

-MAYA ANGELOU-

I Am Never Getting Married

True love arrives from an unexpected place.

This time is important. It's time for you to examine your desires and expectations for love and marriage. Unfortunately, most people don't think carefully about falling in love before they actually do. They mistakenly believe that you have no control over whom you fall in love with, that it's something that just "happens" and you're carried along by it. I want you to take the opportunity now to examine this area of your life. Remember, don't close this book when the writing gets hard.... Keep pushing. This can change your life.

> *First, change your mind. Then, change your life.*

In *Welfare Cheese to Fine Caviar* and in this Companion Guide, I'm candid about the dysfunction surrounding me as I grew up. While some family members did exhibit qualities I wanted to emulate, like Grandma's trustworthiness and Uncle Kendall's work ethic and financial contribution, some of what I saw I was determined to avoid. I wanted no part of alcohol abuse, drug abuse, a lack of higher education, a violent relationship with a woman, or any of the unhealthy patterns and mindsets that would keep me trapped in poverty.

In the last chapter we talked about your trusted few. It is important to have a few people in your life (even one!) who genuinely want the best for you, who want to see you flourish and develop your gifts and talents. A few who have a vision for your future that aligns with your vision—or will even stretch your vision beyond what you can imagine.

A friend once shared with me the counsel her father gave her.

> *Always remember that most people will give you advice based on what's in it for them. They have their own idea of what your life should be like and it's based on something they want or expect from you. It's hard for those people to step back and see your life for what it really could be and give you support for that. They give you the kind of advice and support that is in their favor.*

My friend's dad was right.

At some point, the most influential person in your life will be the one you fall in love with. You will want to share all of life with this special one, and you will want them to be part of the future you dream of. This special one must become one of your trusted few.

When it comes to dating and love and marriage, there are some decisions you must make *in advance*. The emotional highs and lows of a romantic relationship can strip you of your ability to make good decisions. I have seen the old adage "Love is blind" prove itself true. Love (or infatuation) can blind you to what you would otherwise run from.

Read the statements below—it's advice I want you to take to heart. What do you think I mean by each one?

Don't *underestimate* the effect your spouse can have on your life.

Don't *overestimate* the effect your spouse can have on your life.

> I was very careful about how they responded to me and how I responded to them. Did we create violence together or love?

Don't underestimate **the effect your spouse can have on your life.**

If your spouse shares your vision for life and wants to see you flourish in your gifts and talents, they have *tremendous* ability to spur you on and help you structure your life and priorities to accomplish your shared vision.

If your spouse doesn't share your vision for life, seeing you flourish in your gifts and talents will not be a priority for them. They will have *tremendous* ability to discourage you and there will be no vision to work toward together.

Don't overestimate **the effect your spouse can have on your life.**

Some people go into love and marriage believing that their special someone will "make them complete." You must see yourself as "complete" apart from your spouse. No matter how much you love your spouse, no matter how perfectly aligned your goals and dreams are, no matter how much they want to see you flourish…*you* are the only one who can develop your gifts and talents. *You* are the only one who can give your particular gifts to the world. There is much joy in having a wonderful spouse on the journey with you, but you will remain separate "complete" individuals. Your spouse cannot fulfill *your* life's purpose.

IDENTIFY THE REAL FIGHT.

When it comes to love and marriage, the real fight is often against our fears. Take a moment and look inward. What fears do you have about marriage?

_____

_____

_____

_____

Where did those fears come from?

TAKE INVENTORY.

You can overcome fear by being honest about your expectations of marriage and a marriage partner—and setting realistic expectations.

Take a few moments to think deeply about your expectations of marriage. What are your motivations for marriage? What do you believe marriage will bring to your life?

> *The problem was not the girls I was meeting. It was me. My vision of the ideal woman was completely screwed up.*

Take a few moments to think deeply about your vision of the ideal spouse. Describe your ideal spouse.

_____
_____
_____
_____
_____
_____
_____

Now ask yourself: "Where did I get that picture of my ideal spouse?"

_____
_____
_____
_____
_____
_____

Do you believe your expectations of marriage are realistic?

Why or why not?

Do you believe your picture of an ideal spouse is realistic?

Why or why not?

> *I have dated some beautiful people, only to discover that beauty is sometimes skin deep.*

SET YOUR RESOLVE.

Make your decisions about the kind of person you will date or marry *before* you allow someone to get your interest. Make a list of some non-negotiables. I'll get you started by using the list from earlier in this chapter. You'll notice that I use **"I will not date"** statements below. Your marriage relationship will begin with dating, so don't date a person you would not want to marry.

- I will not date a person involved in alcohol or drug abuse.

- I will not date a person who is uninterested in education.

- I will not date a person whose life exemplifies an absence of discipline.

- I will not date a person who shows any sort of violent tendencies.

- I will not date a person with a mindset that keeps them trapped in poverty.

-

-

-

-

-

DO SOMETHING.

Do you know a couple with a happy, healthy marriage? A couple in your circle of family or friends? A couple in your neighborhood or at church?

Who is it?

- Talk to them about their love story. Ask them how they learned to have a healthy marriage, how they support one another, how they make it all work.

- Ask them to share what they consider healthy expectations for marriage.

- Read wonderful books by authors who can serve as marriage mentors. Here are two must-reads:

    » *What Makes a Marriage Last* by Marlo Thomas and Phil Donahue

    » *The 5 Love Languages: The Secret to Love That Lasts* by Gary Chapman

If you don't know a couple with a healthy marriage, don't be discouraged. Not everyone does. Seek out an example of a healthy marriage. Pay attention where you haven't paid attention before—your neighborhood, your church, among your coworkers. When you identify a happy couple, take the same steps listed above!

> "There are plenty of good fish in the sea. You just have to be extremely careful where you stick your fishing pole." —Grandma

CAVIAR TIME

Go to your private space or find a new one. Close and lock the door. Stare at yourself in the mirror. Repeat these words:

"I am blessed and highly favored. I can see my life changing for the better. I have met some great people who have helped me, and others who have strengthened my resolve. I acknowledge that I still have a ways to go.

"I have dated some beautiful people, only to discover that beauty is sometimes skin-deep. When one of them wrongs me, it hurts. I press on because my future is more important than any one person. I trust that God will bring the right person into my life. Until then, I will enjoy meeting new people and having fun.

"This path continues to be difficult at times. Most people close to me do not see the world, much less the future, the way I do. I still love them. In fact, it hurts when I have to distance myself from them or cut them completely off to secure my destiny.

"My dreams of me in possession of my goals are becoming clearer. I can see the path that I need to take. I experience setbacks, but their impact gets weaker each time. Most of the time, they reveal unforeseen paths to success. God is on my side!"

Reflection *Day One*

Let's be honest. Falling in love and pursuing a serious relationship can nurture the vision you have for your life or completely derail it. The one you love can bring out the very best in you—and the very worst. Good, happy marriages are not without challenges, and they don't just happen. So, we're going to dig a little deeper into what's in your mind about marriage and a marriage partner.

This is how change happens!

You know I'm an engineer, so sooner or later I was bound to give you an engineering example. Well, sort of.

Do you know what *reverse engineering* is? Simply put, it's starting with a finished product (software, a machine, aircraft, etc.) and deconstructing it to get the design information from it. In other words, you start with the finished product and work backward to figure out how it was designed so you can recreate it.

Let's start with the "finished product" of your happy, healthy marriage—a life with your spouse that includes a peaceful home and both of you flourishing.

Describe it. What is your home life like? What joint pursuits do you and your spouse have? How do you spend your free time? How do you support one another in reaching your individual goals?

> *Long-term relationships are full of compromises and adjustments.*

Now, work backward and consider what you must have done to design that outcome.

What decisions must you have made?

What relationships must you have pursued?

What or whom must you have avoided?

What must have been your priorities?

When must you have started planning for your success in marriage?

Do you realize you are thinking deeply about keys to a fulfilling life? Most people never give significant time to this. You are. I hope that makes you glad.

Until next time,
Thomas

Reflection *Day Two*

If you flip back through the chapters we've already covered in this guide, you'll see how many topics we've addressed. Obviously, to reach your potential you can't just think about yourself and what you want in life. You have to think deeply and broadly. Education, family dynamics, addiction, values, assumptions, stereotypes, prejudice, discipline...The list goes on as to what you need to discuss and make decisions about. But the two decisions that will have the most impact on your future are how you develop your gifts, talents, and skills—and whom you marry. Nurture your gifts and talents, and nurture your understanding of relationships.

This is how change happens!

Take a moment to review what you've already written in this chapter. As you've examined your thoughts and expectations about marriage and a marriage partner, did you discover that you needed to adjust your thinking? Write about it.

_____

_____

_____

_____

Before we move on, I want to remind you of an essential truth—a safeguard for you to take into every relationship. Actions speak louder than words.

Just say it out loud right now: *actions speak louder than words.*

Always make certain your actions match your words. And expect others to do the same. Especially the one you give your heart to. It doesn't matter how attractive, exciting, financially stable, or talented they are—if they tell you one thing and do another, they are not worthy of you.

> **Do their actions match their words?**

How about your action plan? How are you doing with it? Are you taking steps and investing time to cultivate your gifts, develop your natural talents, and sharpen your skills?

Describe the action steps you're taking. What are you doing? When and how often?

Can you identify improvement? Is your confidence building? Do you feel a bit of excitement?

What about your action steps is easy?

What about your action steps is hard?

> *You can continue a bad cycle in your relationships or you can create your own pattern.*

Have you identified your trusted few? _____

Have you talked with them about your journey and your desire to make the changes necessary to ensure a bright and fulfilling future?

Do you feel their support?

Why or why not?

List one or two action steps that you accomplished last week that you will repeat this week.

List one or two action steps that you have not yet taken. Resolve to take those steps this week.

Your gifts are meant to be cultivated.
Your natural talents are meant to be developed.
Your skills are meant to be sharpened.
And you are the only one who can do it.

You've got this! Until next time,
Thomas

> *"Potential means nothing if you don't do anything with it."*
>
> -EVAN CARMICHAEL-

Control Your Response

Inaction is often the best reaction to crazies, especially those in authority.

This time is important. It's time for you to learn the value of self-awareness and embrace self-discipline. You can't have one without the other, and the development of your gifts depends on both. Remember, don't close this book when the writing gets hard.... Keep pushing. This can change your life.

> *First, change your mind. Then, change your life.*

One of the most important gifts you can give to yourself is self-awareness—fully knowing who you are, what you do, and how you think. Self-awareness requires that you investigate your internal beliefs and look at the influences of your upbringing and environment, but only to discover *reasons*—not *excuses*. Self-awareness offers opportunity for growth and change because it enables you to honestly evaluate your strengths and weaknesses.

In *Welfare Cheese to Fine Caviar*, I share an important chapter in my life when self-awareness enabled me to make a life-changing decision. With two scholarships standing ready to pave the way for a college education, I chose a different path and joined the United States Army Reserve after high school.

Three of my relatives had enlisted in the military. I had witnessed the positive change it brought to them. They became men of discipline, a kind of discipline that would serve them well for the rest of their lives. I knew myself well enough to know that, despite a stellar high school academic record, I lacked the kind of discipline I admired in them.

What does *discipline* mean to you?

As you described what *discipline* means to you, did you think of positive things or negative?

Discipline tends to conjure up negative images and thoughts for many people. Probably because it's confused with *punishment*. They are two different concepts.

Punishment is an undesirable consequence received for doing something wrong. It comes from *outside* of you and is intended to prevent you from repeating a behavior. *Discipline* is a character trait that enables your success. It comes from *inside* of you and enables you to accomplish a goal.

I want you to make friends with discipline. And to make sure the concept is clear, let's use the word *self-discipline*.

Years ago, I heard someone say that self-discipline is the ability to do *what* needs to be done *when* it needs to be done. That's a pretty good definition, but let's add a little more to it.

Self-discipline is the ability to do *what* needs to be done *when* it needs to be done, understanding *why* it needs to be done.

In order to develop self-discipline that will serve you well for the rest of your life, it's not enough to know the *what* and *when* of each endeavor. That's too much like simply following instructions. You must understand the *why*. The *why* component speaks to your internal motivation, keeps the big picture in mind, and enables you to transfer self-discipline to every area of life.

> **What will you do when faced with challenges?**

IDENTIFY THE REAL FIGHT.

What are the challenges you face when it comes to self-discipline?

TAKE INVENTORY.

Self-discipline is not about being rigid or harsh. It's about combining self-awareness and intentionality. It's what you do when no one else is looking. It's about aligning your schedule, activities, and effort with your goals. It's about actually making your goals your priority. "What?" you may be asking. "My goals already *are* my priority!"

Hmm. Are they?

Having a goal doesn't automatically make that goal a priority. Most goals get only lip service. Not action.

Think about yesterday. Or today, if you're doing this at night. What did you do? Seriously. Think about the progression of your day and describe what you did.

Okay, let's get real. What do you see about your use of your time? In addition to the day you just described, think about this past week. This past month. How did you use your time? How much time did you invest in your goals? How much time did you spend on entertainment? How much time did you give to your work?

You can determine what your priorities are by examining how you use your time. That's being self-aware. If you use up hours scrolling through Facebook or Instagram and very little time working on a goal, you've in essence made Facebook or Instagram (which is entertainment) your priority—no matter what you *say* is your goal. Remember, your actions speak louder than your words.

What percentage of time are you investing in developing your gifts and talents?

How does that compare with the amount of time you're using up on activities that don't matter? Okay, let me ask it frankly: How much time are you wasting?

Which is greater: the amount of time you invest in developing your gifts and talents or the amount of time you waste?

Your time is precious. You are allotted the same daily amount as every other human on the planet. Time can never be retrieved. Use it wisely.

SET YOUR RESOLVE.

I said earlier that self-discipline is about combining self-awareness and intentionality. Spend a few moments thinking about this. You know your strengths and weaknesses. You know what you *say* your priorities are, and you know how you use your time. You also know that nothing will change until you align your schedule, activities, and effort with your goals—actually making your goals your priority.

Be your own compassionate friend, and write what you need to hear right now.

Prepare yourself mentally.

DO SOMETHING.

Look again at what you recorded about your use of time. Think through a better investment of your day. Write a plan here. I've included a couple of examples.

On my ride to work   Listen to motivational podcast

Lunch break   Practice sketching

5:30–6:15 p.m.   Complete online lesson on charcoal sketching

We are creatures of habit.

CAVIAR TIME

Go to your private space or find a new one. Close and lock the door. Stare at yourself in the mirror. Repeat these words:

"God continues to throw difficult tests at me. At times, I want to quit and take the easier path. But I know that He doesn't test me on anything that He has not already prepared me for. The more I overcome, the stronger I get.

"I have experienced times when it has been extremely difficult to not respond by punching, slapping, or hurling cuss words at someone. I know that I would not be fighting them alone. Society does not see my vision and potential, nor cares. Instead, society is waiting in the background for me to slip, so that I can be placed in jail if I am lucky. I am not the person they see in their stereotype. God, please forgive them for they know not what they do.

"God is shaping me into someone who will have a positive impact on society. I will help improve the lives of ALL, regardless of their perception of me. The more people I help, the greater the blessings that God gives me. No one will stand between success and me!"

Reflection *Day One*

I hope you're smiling. I hope you realize how far you've come on this journey. How much you've considered that you haven't given attention to before. I'm smiling as I write this, because I know what it's like to have light break through the darkness. If I were with you in person right now, I'd say, "You've got this! Keep going. Keep doing the hard work. Invest in yourself."

This is how change happens!

Most people respond to advice about self-discipline with one of two reactions:

- An exaggerated eye roll that says, "Here we go again. Can't we talk about something else?"

Or

- A deep sigh that releases "I've tried a hundred times and I just can't do it" anxiety

But not you! From this point forward, I want you to embrace any mention of self-discipline because you'll be equipped with personal experience and insight to add to the conversation.

Write down a few positive words that you now connect with *self-discipline*.

> *They became very disciplined people. Role models.*

Now, think through it this way: What does self-discipline bring with it?

_____

_____

_____

_____

_____

_____

Did you include words like *stability, order, structure, opportunity, hope, self-satisfaction*? Think deeply and add a few more words.

> *What will be the first thing you do when you reach your goal? How will you celebrate your sacrifices?*

The process of developing self-discipline isn't easy. Whether you're enduring the "close attention" of a drill sergeant, studying for exams, or revising a business proposal for the fifth time, there will come a moment when you'll want to quit. That's the moment to remind yourself of the *why* of the task at hand, to allow the big picture to fuel your internal motivation. And keep going.

Say this out loud:

If I am to reach my goals for my future, I must embrace self-discipline.

> *If I am to embrace self-discipline, I must keep my eyes on my goals for my future.*

What do those statements mean to you?

Until next time,
Thomas

Reflection *Day Two*

You are developing qualities that will carry you into the future you desire. You value self-awareness and embrace self-discipline. You understand that you are in control of your responses, and you won't forfeit that control to anyone.

This is how change happens!

In the chapter "Control Your Response," I describe my first encounter with Drill Sergeant Collins, whose only apparent goal was to provoke me into a fight. "You're from the hood, aren't you?" he barked as he ordered me to the top floor of the barracks where we'd be alone. He goaded me, trying to provoke a response.

> *It's just me and you right now. Just me and you.*
> *I can see it on your face.*
>
> *You want to fight me. If you want to fight,*
> *you can do whatever.*
>
> *It's just me and you. I'm going to take this hat off.*
> *We can go at it right now.*

I can only imagine what would have happened if I had allowed his insults and taunting to get the best of me. But I didn't. Somehow I knew my future in the Reserve was riding on my response.

Years earlier, a group of friends singled me out to "handle" a guy they accused of calling us the N-word after one of our group instigated the name-calling. Even after the guy pulled out a knife and lunged at me, I was expected to fight him for revenge. I can only imagine what would have happened if I had caved in to my friends' coercion. But I didn't. Somehow I knew their wrath would be easier to deal with than the outcome of that fight.

Have you ever been intentionally provoked? Have you ever been coerced to respond in an inappropriate way? Describe the incident(s).

How did you respond?

Not long after I refused to fight the guy with the knife, I encountered him again. This time he was on the same church bus as me, going to Hampton Park Baptist. Imagine that. We went from a scary situation that included a knife to riding the church bus together every week.

As it turned out, Drill Sergeant Collins was one of the most admired drill sergeants at Fort McClellan in Anniston, Alabama. I came to think the world of him because, as I write in my book, "he put even greater effort into building me into a strong soldier and man than he did breaking me down. The yelling and screaming turned into encouragement, respect, and compliments when he noticed I was giving all that I had."

You are always in control of your own response. You have that ability—that *response*-ability to be in control. Don't yield that control to anyone.

Think of the person you identified in an earlier chapter, the one who looks to you as a role model. How would you explain to them the importance of self-awareness, self-discipline, and response-ability?

> "Pukey, if you make your bed hard, you have to sleep in it." —Grandma

Now, how are you doing with your action plan? Are you taking steps and investing time to cultivate your gifts, develop your natural talents, and sharpen your skills?

What positive steps have you taken in the past few days?

Have you adjusted your use of time since examining your schedule in this chapter? What adjustments have you made?

If you haven't made any adjustments, why not? Is it because you are doing well investing time in developing your gifts and talents? Are you having trouble knowing what adjustments to make?

> *If I feel that I need something to achieve a goal, I am not too shy to go after it... I will do it because that's what it takes.*

List one action step that you accomplished in the past few days that you will repeat in the next few.

List one action step that you have not yet taken. Resolve to take that step before another week has passed.

Value self-awareness.
Embrace self-discipline.
Don't forfeit your response-ability.

You've got this! Until next time,
Thomas

> *"Change is hard at first, messy in the middle and gorgeous at the end."*
>
> -ROBIN SHARMA-

The Payoff

The pathway to earning more while working less lies in your head.

This time is important. It's time for you to think about the moment that will mark the start of a new life for you…the moment when all your hard work and dreams come together. But before that moment comes, there'll be plenty more opportunities for self-examination, more need for soul-searching, more call for careful planning, and more necessary action steps. Don't be overwhelmed. Enjoy the amazing journey into your future. Remember, don't close this book when the writing gets hard.…Keep pushing. This can change your life.

> *First, change your mind.*
> *Then, change your life.*

"I made it. I finally made." On the day that you say these words, what will you have accomplished? What will these words mean to you? Describe it.

For me, it was the day I graduated from college with a job waiting for me. It was *the* job—the one I'd hoped for, at the salary I desired, in the city where I wanted to be. I marked that moment as the start of my new life.

What about you? What is the moment that will mark the start of your new life?

Who do you want to share that moment with you?

What will you say to them?

I want to tell you this: you're going to get there. You're going to arrive at that moment that marks the start of your new life. Why do I know? Because you're changing your life *now*. You're looking inward, becoming more self-aware, and developing the self-discipline that will grow your gifts and talents. If you keep going, you'll arrive at your moment.

In *Welfare Cheese to Fine Caviar*, I write about an "elevator pitch." Do you remember what it is? It's an engaging way to introduce yourself and describe what you do, intended to gain the support of someone you've never met in the thirty seconds you have with them in an elevator. Here's an example:

> *I'm Thomas Wideman and I recently graduated from college with a degree in chemical engineering. I'm completing an internship with Parkland Chemical Corporation and have discovered two things: I'm strong at process engineering and I love the Southeast. So I'm looking for an engineering job in this region.*

Now, imagine yourself in an elevator. The elevator stops and someone you've never met steps in. You recognize this person as someone who could connect you to an opportunity. "Hello," they greet you. "I don't believe we've met."

It's time for your elevator pitch. Write it here.

There came a moment when I realized my future was up to me, but only if I made vastly different choices in the present.

Now it's time for self-awareness. Let's call it brutal honesty.

What if your elevator pitch described exactly how you are investing your time right now? (Remember the exercise from the last chapter?) Go ahead. Write it.

Here's what I want you to examine. Could you honestly give an elevator pitch that includes something like:

> *I want to be a book illustrator, so I'm investing two hours a day in developing my talent for sketching.*
>
> *I'm interested in finance, so I've enrolled in a cryptocurrency course that is beyond what is required for my major.*
>
> *I've just begun a mentoring relationship with a woman who's an expert in my field of interest.*

Given the self-awareness called for in this exercise, would your elevator pitch have to include anything like:

> *I want to be a landscaper, but I'm too busy right now to pursue it.*

I can see myself teaching piano after performing for a few years. Music theory has always come easily for me, so I don't feel particularly compelled to spend much time on it.

I know I need to spend more time developing my writing skills, but you know how it is. I check Instagram and the next thing you know, it's two hours later!

Let's write one more elevator pitch with *this* scenario: You are focused on your goals and excited about your future. You are investing in yourself on a regular (if not daily) basis, developing your gifts and talents with your future in mind. Now, write *that* elevator pitch.

Two more questions for today:

- Is the final elevator pitch you wrote a fair description of how you are investing your life right now?

- And what do you need to say to yourself about that?

> *More than anything, I wanted to make something of myself. To make good on that determination from my childhood.*

CAVIAR TIME

Go to your private space or find a new one. Close and lock the door. Stare at yourself in the mirror. Repeat these words:

"Wow. My blood, sweat, and tears have paid off. I am extremely thankful. There were so many times that I wanted to quit and take the easier path. But I pressed on when I was tired, hurt, or discouraged.

"I realize that I have not done this on my own. *So* many people have helped me. Although I cannot afford to repay them —none of them would accept payment if I tried—I will pay it forward by encouraging others to achieve their dreams.

"Though my journey is not over, I realize that I have all that I need to be successful. I am smart. I am handsome/beautiful. I know how to gain the skills that I don't possess. The scars of my past, both emotional and physical, have become my impenetrable armor.

"I cannot explain a lot of things that have happened to me. Unexpected and unrequested aid arrive at my time of need, tense encounters miraculously diffuse overnight without my involvement, and heavenly oversight has been sent at times when I was being reckless. There are so many traps. Avoiding pregnancies, diseases, arrests, fights, expulsions, and fines are challenging, especially when society expects that from you. How am I alive, free, and living well today?

Thank you, God!"

Reflection *Day One*

I'm proud of you. Proud of your willingness to do what it takes to reach the future of your dreams. I'm thankful too. Thankful that you've allowed me to share my story in order to encourage you. I said this at the outset, and I mean it: every struggle I've ever faced will have been worth it if I can help you reach the future of your dreams.

This is how change happens!

IDENTIFY THE REAL FIGHT.

We had some fun with the elevator pitch, but I do hope that it pushed you to think deeply and look honestly at how you are investing your days. If you're having difficulty, what is the real battle behind a regular pattern of days that show no evidence of your goals, no investment in your gifts or talents?

If you're investing your days well—bravo! Have you identified any situation you must avoid or habit you must keep in check to stay on track? Write about it here. And keep drawing on your self-discipline to move forward.

> *"Pukey, the devil will always test you when you are doing something good."* —Grandma

TAKE INVENTORY.

Lean on your self-awareness. Talk with one of your trusted few. Look at your calendar and your habits. What do you need to adjust in order to have an elevator pitch that you'll be excited to share—an elevator pitch that describes a motivated, self-disciplined individual enjoying the process of developing their gifts and talents in preparation for a wonderful future that is well within their grasp?

SET YOUR RESOLVE.

How are you doing? Are you motivated? That's great. Take a moment and write about how you keep your resolve.

Are you discouraged? That's okay. You are human, and there is an ebb and flow to life and progress. Why do you think your resolve waivers? Talk with one of your trusted few, and ask them to help you put everything in perspective.

> *Celebrate the small wins and learn from the failures along the way.*

DO SOMETHING.

On an index card, write the elevator pitch that you'd be excited to share—the one that describes a motivated, self-disciplined individual enjoying the process of developing their gifts and talents in preparation for a wonderful future that is well within their grasp!

Now take that elevator pitch card and

- tape it to your mirror,
- take a screenshot and make it the wallpaper on your phone,
- read it to your trusted few,
- memorize it,
- pattern your days after it.

Until next time,
Thomas

Reflection *Day Two*

You're about to complete another chapter in this companion devoted to guiding you to the future you dream of. You are engaging in thoughtful discussions, learning about yourself, and writing down your insights. You're doing it even though you don't have to. But then again…I think you *do* have to. I'm guessing there's an inner voice urging you on, an internal spark that glows brightly at the thought of reaching your goals, a self-awareness that confirms you do indeed have what it takes to succeed! Pay attention to your inner nudging.…Keep believing in yourself.

This is how change happens!

Let's do a different kind of reflection today. Spend a few moments looking back over what you've already completed in your Companion Guide. Maybe you're like me and draw stars to emphasize important points or use highlighters to mark passages to come back to again and again. Maybe you write in the margins or dog-ear pages. Whatever you do to make this book your own, let that be your guide as you review what you've already read and written.

- Spend some time meditating on what has been most important to you, and why.
- Write additional thoughts or insights that come to mind.
- Reread your favorite quotes.
- Mark a passage that you'd like to read to one of your trusted few. Or go ahead and text it to them.
- Finally, read again your descriptions of your gifts and natural talents and skills. They are part of who you are. Don't neglect them.

You've got this! Until next time,
Thomas

> "I am not a product of my circumstances. I am a product of my decisions."
>
> -STEPHEN R. COVEY-

Life is Short. Live It Well.

I did not have a heart attack,
but I wasn't so sure at the time.

This time is important. It's time for you to think about a variety of issues that are interrelated—embracing difficulty, good stress and bad stress, self-care, and your perspective on success. It's not for the faint of heart, but it's part of the amazing journey into your future. Remember, don't close this book when the writing gets hard.... Keep pushing. This can change your life.

> *First, change your mind. Then, change your life.*

Difficulty is a staple of life. Challenges are common. Obstacles will often seem to outweigh opportunities. They are to be expected—even embraced. As the Chinese proverb says, "The gem cannot be polished without friction, nor man perfected without trials."

There was a season in my life when challenges seemed to come at me from everywhere. From the outside looking in on my life, you would have seen a successful businessman living his dream with a beautiful wife and children and prospering in his career. But the truth was, I was in distress.

At work, I was leading a team and managing a multimillion-dollar budget as part of a 1.2-billion-dollar project. But I was also dealing with a supervisor who was seemingly intent on seeing me fail. My supervisor went beyond disrespecting me to treating me in such a way that caused some of the white male employees to express their shame at his behavior. He undermined my instructions to my team, changed assignments and scope of work, stopped tasks before they were completed, and kept me in the dark on his decisions. His behavior could have cost me my job and the company millions.

Things weren't good at home either. Melanie and I were struggling and starting to grow apart. There wasn't an area of my life that was smooth and easy.

I'm sharing this with you for a reason. There's something I want you to know. If you continue the journey you've started, you'll reach your goals. You'll live the future you dream of. But you'll never get to a place where every area of your life is always smooth and easy.

But I want you to know something else.

Difficulties do not have to discourage you, challenges do not have to conquer you, and obstacles need not overwhelm you. They all carry with them the possibility of your personal growth. They offer a new way of refining your character and sharpening your outlook. They provide a catalyst for propelling you forward, for making needed adjustments, and for identifying an area in need of attention.

Life is unpredictable. It involves people and circumstances out of your control.

You *will* have difficulties. You *will* be met with challenges. You *will* encounter obstacles. I want you to be well quipped to face them.

As you read about the difficult season I encountered, did it remind you of a season in your life? Describe it.

The difficult season I just shared with you culminated in a heart attack scare. From the ambulance ride through the hospital stay, I was completely out of control. I had no certainty about the outcome and no ability to change any damage that had already been done to my body.

Thankfully (and despite the initial deduction by the emergency room doctor), I did not suffer a heart attack. While I never want to go through that experience again, I consider those days in the hospital a gift. I was forced to stop, to sit with the truth, and take a hard look at areas in my life that needed adjustment.

> The path to your goal is not always a straight line.

As important as financial stability was to me, what flooded my thoughts during that hospital stay wasn't money. It was people. It was Melanie and my boys. *How am I doing as a husband? How can I listen to Melanie better? How am I doing as a dad? Am I raising my boys right?* It was family, friends, and coworkers. *Am I treating them well? Do I show them respect?* It was people I'd never even met, people who'd been brought up in poverty like me that I wanted to help and encourage. *I know I have a purpose. I have to share my story.*

Family. Friends. People. They are the real treasures in life.

Stop for a moment. Who are your treasures?

While that season of my life did not include a heart attack, it did include a change of heart. No matter how much we'd like to be, we are *never* completely in control of our lives or our circumstances. However, we *are* always in control of our perspective. That hospital stay offered me a chance to examine my perspective.

Do you agree that we're never completely in control of our lives or our circumstances? What are your thoughts?

What does "perspective" mean to you?

Do you believe you are always in control of your perspective? Why or why not?

During my hospital stay, my perspective shifted. The idea of success came more clearly into focus. I understood that success cannot be one-dimensional. It is much more about what I *give* than what I *get*. I realized I couldn't call achievement "success" if it came at the expense of my health or my family's well-being. I decided that my pursuit of success would always include boundaries to protect myself and my family.

I'd like to share with you the thoughts that crystallized as I made adjustments to bring balance to my life. My hope is that, as you pursue your dreams and reach your goals, you'll measure success as much by what you give as by what you achieve. Here's what success includes for me.

GIVE LOVE, RESPECT, AND KINDNESS.

Success for me includes consistently giving love, respect, and kindness to the people around me—no matter how I am being treated. Every person I meet is a person of value. As a human being, they have inherent dignity and worth, and they deserve my respect. Another's disrespectful behavior toward me does not justify my own disrespectful behavior. I won't tear others down; I'll try to lift them up.

I've set a boundary. I won't require myself to remain in a situation where I am continually disrespected and mistreated.

> *"Kill them with kindness."* —Grandma

GIVE MORE THAN IS EXPECTED.

Success for me includes giving more than what is expected. This means the effort I give doesn't stop at the minimum requirements.

Instead of
"I'll give what's required because I have to"
my attitude will be
"I'll give more because I want to."

I'll not say to my coworkers,
"I'll give the minimum because that's enough."
I'll say,
"I'll give more because I value you and I value our common goal."

My relationships will not thrive with
"I'll give what's expected to satisfy you."

I'll nurture my relationships with
"I'll give more because that's what you deserve."

I've set boundaries. I will not give beyond my capacity to maintain my health and my family's well-being. I will not give beyond reason and cause myself to burn out. Giving *more* does not mean giving *everything*. And I will not allow my giving to enable someone else to neglect their responsibilities.

GIVE ENCOURAGEMENT AND SUPPORT.

Success for me includes giving encouragement and support to others. It means sharing my story to help someone else realize their potential. It means encouraging others to cultivate their gifts, develop their talents, and sharpen their skills. It means sharing the lessons I've learned to help another reach the future they dream of.

I've set a boundary. I remember that every individual is responsible for their own gifts, talents, and skills. Every individual is responsible for doing the hard work of pursuing their goals. I can't do it for them, and I won't attempt to.

GIVE CARE TO MYSELF.

Success for me includes giving care to myself. A heart attack scare gave me a taste of what happens when self-care is neglected. Self-care includes the essentials we're often reminded of:

- A nutritious diet
- Regular exercise
- Plenty of sleep
- Relaxation and fun

Self-care also requires self-awareness and includes crucial elements we don't often hear about:

- Setting boundaries
- Maintaining healthy relationships
- Sharpening our mind
- Recognizing the different kinds of stress

I've set boundaries. I prioritize self-care and will not consider it non-essential. Self-care is not selfish. By caring for myself, I make sure I'm able to care for my family and I set a good example for them.

> Spending two days face-to-face with your own mortality will certainly give you a new perspective on things.

IDENTIFY THE REAL FIGHT.

You will always have an internal struggle, you'll always run the risk of wounding relationships, and you'll toy with neglecting your well-being if you have an unrealistic or unhealthy view of success.

Take a moment to consider your perspective on success. Don't write what you think you *should* write. Be brutally honest with yourself. Right now, how do you view success? Can you define it? What does it include for you?

TAKE INVENTORY.

Take another look at what you just wrote. Do you have a realistic and healthy view of success?

Is your view of a successful future one-dimensional? Do you define it by only one accomplishment or focus on only one area of your life? Look at what you wrote—what do you see there?

SET YOUR RESOLVE.

An unhealthy view of success can set you up for failure. Determine to cultivate a healthy view of success. When you think of your future, think of all the components of your life. Don't focus on one area at the expense of another.

DO SOMETHING.

Be intentional in cultivating a healthy view of success. Here are a few ideas.

- Read good books and broaden your reading. For instance, don't just read books about achieving financial success. Read books about healthy relationships, marriage, and parenting. Read about conflict management and personality types. Read about setting boundaries. Read about health and nutrition. Read about how to keep your brain sharp. You get the point! And be sure to look in the back of *Welfare Cheese to Fine Caviar* for the bibliography and "Other Great Books in My Library."

- Spend some time with one or more of your trusted few and talk about success. Share with them what you've read and written.

- Identify someone you respect and view as "successful." Ask if you can spend a little time with them. You will honor them by your request. Ask them about their view of success, challenges they face to keep life in balance, and what they've learned about success.

Make your action plan for cultivating a healthy view of success.

What new subject will you read about next?

And what will the next subject be?

Which of your trusted few will you contact first to have some great conversation about success? And when will you contact them? (How about right now?!)

What successful person will you ask to spend time with? And when will you contact them?

We've covered a lot today. Well done!

> *God gave me that time alone to sit with the truth so I could be more careful in my next steps.*

CAVIAR TIME

Go to your private space or find a new one. Close and lock the door. Stare at yourself in the mirror. Repeat these words:

"God, I have proven to society that I belong. I have taken all their punches and insults and converted them into positive energy. Yet, they still test me. Still insult me. Still mistreat me. Still ignore me.

"Life continues to be a constant test of my faith in people, religion, government, and self. But I have faith in YOU. You have gotten me this far, and I know You have great plans for me. Honestly, the little games that people play now are not as serious as the life-threatening ones growing up. No fists, knives, guns, or extreme emotions are involved.

"Regardless of how people treat me, I will treat them with respect and love. I will give more than what is expected of me on my job, sports, or other activities that I am involved in. I will influence and support people in achieving their goals because I know what You have brought me through. I will take time to exercise, relax, and celebrate the journey with my loved ones because life is precious and time is limited. I will take, and enjoy, the high road!"

Reflection *Day One*

I just Googled "determination" and was rewarded with a wonderful definition: *firmness of purpose*. I like what that expresses. *You* are exhibiting an amazing firmness of purpose. We are meeting here on Reflection Day One after you've invested a great deal of time and effort on this journey. You're still reading, still thinking deeply, and still writing. *You* are doing the hard work. I'm proud of you. Today, we're doing a deep dive into the topic of stress.

This is how change happens!

Stress is normal. Like difficulty, it's a staple of life. We experience stress as emotional or physical tension—our body's reaction to a challenge or demand, an event, or even a thought.[1] There's good stress and bad stress. Good stress makes us mentally and physically stronger; it enhances our productivity. Bad stress can land us in the hospital. You need to know the difference between the good and the bad.

Consider this Reflection Day a crash course in stress. Before we start, describe how you typically respond when you're under stress. How does your body feel?

---

1. A.D.A.M. *Medical Encyclopedia*, s.v. "Stress and Your Health," February 16, 2021 https://medlineplus.gov/ency/article/003211.htm.

What happens to you emotionally?

Now, let me introduce you to what I call the "Stress Quartet"—Eustress, Acute Stress, Chronic Stress, and Distress. For this section, I've leaned heavily on the article "Am I Stressed or in Distress?" by Ashley Addiction Treatment.[1]

EUSTRESS

Eustress is considered good for us. It's the kind of stress we experience when we're interviewing for a job, starting college, or moving to a new city. Eustress works to our advantage, releasing hormones into our body that heighten our motivation and productivity. It helps us persevere through mental and physical challenges, making us emotionally and physically stronger. Don't be concerned about eustress.

List a few times you've recently experienced eustress.

---

1. "Am I Stressed or in Distress?" Ashley Addiction Treatment, April 6, 2020, https://www.ashleytreatment.org/the-difference-between-stress-and-distress/.

ACUTE STRESS

Acute stress is a one-off or short-term stress that quickly goes away. It's what happens when we're startled awake by a fire alarm or have a heated argument. Acute stress helps us manage dangerous situations like avoiding a car accident. We experience it when we do something exciting like ride a roller coaster or take our first leap off a diving board. Acute stress releases hormones (like adrenaline) into our body that can cause anxiety, shortness of breath, and headaches. These effects are unpleasant but when the stressor is over, our body returns to normal. Don't be concerned about acute stress.

When have you recently experienced acute stress?

CHRONIC STRESS

Chronic stress crosses the line into bad stress. Unresolved stress that continues for weeks or months is chronic stress. It's what we experience when we have an unhealthy marriage or ongoing financial problems. The prolonged and excessive release of stress hormones caused by chronic stress can result in serious health issues, such as increased risk of stroke, heart trouble, a compromised immune system, and chronic pain. Chronic stress can also result in mental health issues like panic attacks and depression. One of the dangers of chronic stress is that the unresolved situation can go on so long that we get used to what we're experiencing. We don't realize that our "normal" isn't normal—or that our physical and mental well-being are at stake. Be concerned about chronic stress.

Do you recognize your own experience in the description of chronic stress? Can you write about it?

DISTRESS

We are thrust into *distress* when the amount of stress we are experiencing is greater than our ability to manage it. Chronic stress often becomes distress, which is entirely negative. Causes of distress are not confined to external factors. We can be in distress when we're unable to manage our internal stressors, such as fear, obsessive thought patterns, and perfectionism. Be very concerned about distress.

Can you recall a time when you've been in distress? If the distress has passed and the situation causing it has been resolved, write about that experience. How did the distress affect you physically and emotionally? How was it resolved?

> *I would argue that a certain level of stress is good for you... however, this was the first time it had affected my health.*

Here's a very important question: Are you in distress now?

If you are in distress, you need to be concerned. The stress you're experiencing is greater than you're ability to manage it. **Please—right away—take action:**

- Get to a doctor.
- Talk to one of your trusted few. Don't go through this without support.
- Ask for help to manage the stress and get the situation resolved. It may mean seeing a counselor or therapist, seeking financial help or advice, making significant lifestyle changes, or meeting with a supervisor. Don't try to figure it out by yourself. Don't keep it to yourself.
- Take it seriously. Don't wait.

Be self-aware. Recognize your external and internal stressors and the different types of stress. Take action to manage your stress before you are thrust into distress. Keep an eye on your family and friends. If you see signs of distress, be their advocate.

Until next time,
Thomas

Reflection *Day Two*

You are winding up another chapter, and this one has been intense. You are learning that success is not one-dimensional. The life of your dreams is about much more than developing your gifts. It calls for *knowledge* (what you learn) and *wisdom* (how you apply what you learn for the benefit of yourself and others). Today, we're looking at two areas that require knowledge and wisdom: self-care and your perspective on success.

This is how change happens!

Self-care is a critical component to managing stress and avoiding distress. Take a look at the lists below. You'll recognize them from earlier in this chapter.

Self-care includes the essentials we're often reminded of:

- A nutritious diet
- Regular exercise
- Plenty of sleep
- Relaxation and fun

How are you doing with these essentials of self-care?

> **Life is too short.**

Self-care requires self-awareness and includes these crucial elements:

- Setting boundaries
- Maintaining healthy relationships
- Sharpening our mind
- Recognizing the different kinds of stress

How are you doing with these elements of self-care?

List two elements of self-care you want to learn more about. Then look for a book!

One more thing. Have you given more thought to your perspective on success? Without looking at what you wrote previously, describe what success means for you. Have you developed your definition?

You've got this! Until next time,
Thomas

"Only I can change my life. No one can do it for me."

-CAROL BURNETT-

Sharpen Your Focus

*When your motivation or focus is low,
help someone else achieve their goals.*

This time is important. It's time for you to consider what to do when you've lost your inner drive. It's time to pull together all you're learning in a plan that will help you move forward when the going gets tough. This is part of preparing for the future you dream of. Remember, don't close this book when the writing gets hard…. Keep pushing. This can change your life.

> *First, change your mind. Then, change your life.*

At some point in the future, you'll find yourself unenthused, complacent, without focus, low on motivation, and disinterested in setting goals. How do I know? Because it happened to me. And it didn't happen years ago when I was just getting started. It happened fairly recently. It happened after I had achieved every goal I'd set out to accomplish. It happened while I was reaping the rewards of diligently pursuing my dreams. It happened after I'd been married nearly two decades. After I'd had two wonderful sons. It happened years after I'd written the first manuscript of *Welfare Cheese to Fine Caviar.* It just happened. And do you know why?

It happened because I'm human.

I was internally driven, forward-thinking, and self-motivated to pursue my goals. It made no sense to me that I lost my inner fire. I was moving—but I wasn't really going anywhere.

Are you internally driven and self-motivated to pursue your goals? How would you describe yourself right now?

_____

_____

_____

_____

Have you already experienced a season—after achieving some major success and meeting important goals—when you lost motivation and focus? Were you disinterested in setting goals and pursuing your dreams? What was it like?

_____

_____

_____

_____

_____

Were you able to move beyond it and regain motivation and focus? How?

I call a season like this "burnout." Experiencing it is normal. Burnout can take over for a number of reasons. Perhaps we've pushed hard for a long time and we're just physically or mentally drained. Or maybe we've pushed so hard in an unhealthy way and have worked ourselves into burnout. Someone's negative opinion or negative influence may bring on burnout. Or we may have welcomed it by neglecting self-care.

I came out of my burnout by pulling together many lessons I'd learned over the years. But the key component I had not anticipated was the fulfillment of a dream my wife, Melanie, had. In *Welfare Cheese to Fine Caviar,* I share Melanie's dream and how it came to fruition. Watching her pursue her dream and investing in that dream with her refueled my own fire. Passion and purpose can be contagious. Look around. Whose passion may refuel your own?

> *Her victory will be our victory.*

As always, I want you to shorten your journey by learning from mine. So, here's a plan for navigating burnout. As you've already learned, thinking honestly and deeply through the subjects and questions is the key. Your answers will help you discover your path out of burnout.

SPECIAL INSTRUCTIONS: If you are currently in burnout, grab a separate notebook and go through this exercise now.

DO A SELF-AWARENESS CHECK

Remember that self-awareness is a gift to yourself. Always start here.

- Am I experiencing stress or distress?
- What tendencies do I have that are contributing to my burnout?
- Do I need to ask my trusted few to help me see my blindspots?

OBJECTIVELY ASSESS THE CAUSES

As we consider the causes of burnout, we won't be looking for a place to put the blame. We'll look for clues to the corrections—signposts to the solutions.

- Am I being drained by circumstances?
- Am I being drained by a person?
- Am I discouraged by someone's opinion, feedback, or influence?

DO A SELF-EVALUATION

While self-awareness focuses on knowledge of your inner self, self-evaluation looks at your actions.

- Am I taking care of my body?
- Am I taking care of myself mentally?
- Are my close relationships healthy?
- Am I setting boundaries to protect myself and my family?

LOOK FOR INSPIRATION FROM THE PEOPLE IN YOUR LIFE

- Who speaks into my life with love and clarity?
- Who can I talk to about my burnout?
- Who can I encourage?
- Who can I help?
- Whose passion will refuel my own?

We're doing a little something different here. You'll see below the phrases for the process you've been guided through a number of times already. You're used to thinking deeply about the issues we discuss, and you've learned valuable skills as we've been on this journey together. You're ready to guide yourself through this process. Review what you've read and written today. What is speaking to you? Use the process for what you know you need.

Identify the real fight.

Take inventory.

Set your resolve.

Do something.

From time to time, you will lose focus or the energy to push forward... Don't panic. You're human.

CAVIAR TIME

Go to your private space or find a new one. Close and lock the door. Stare at yourself in the mirror. Repeat these words:

"Relax. I have achieved more than I would have ever dreamed before. Have I celebrated my achievements along the way? (Smile.) I will celebrate them now.

"Reflect. What is my purpose? What am I doing now to achieve it? What is driving me? Have I steered off course?

"Renew. Who can I help achieve their goals? My spouse? My children? My friends? My coworkers? Or a random stranger?

"Restart. I am back on track. Helping others has reinvigorated me. God is great!"

Reflection *Day One*

I've said this before, and I'm saying it again: I'm proud of you. I imagine you didn't expect to delve into some of the topics we've covered. Every one of them is important to your success. When you invest time to understand their importance, you are equipping yourself for your future. Today, we're going to talk about learning from other successful people. You need to be intentional about it.

This is how change happens!

In the last chapter, you identified a person you consider to be successful.

Who is it?

What do you see in them that you admire?

How many different areas of their life do you have knowledge of?

Have you contacted them to ask to spend time with them?

If you haven't, what's holding you back?

> *Every great change in my life was preceded by a low point.*

Don't skip this action step. Learning from others is critical to achieving your dreams. If this pushes you outside your comfort zone, that's good—growth never happens in there!

Write down some questions you'd like to ask this person. I'm confident they'll be honored to encourage you and share what they've learned.

Now, if you feel safe enough to share your fears with this person, what would you share?

Let me encourage you—go ahead and share your fears. Chances are very good that this person you obviously respect will have had those same fears. And they'll be able to tell you how they overcame them.

Until next time,
Thomas

Reflection *Day Two*

You're about to complete another chapter in this guide to the future you dream of. My hope is that, with every completed chapter, your confidence and belief in yourself is growing. I hope you're living with an excitement about your future. More than that, an excitement about your life right now as you discover more about who you are and the gifts you have to give to the world. We're going to revisit some things today and see how you're doing.

This is how change happens!

Remember the elevator pitch you wrote for "The Payoff"? It's the one you'd be excited to share—the one that describes a motivated, self-disciplined individual enjoying the process of developing their gifts and talents in preparation for a wonderful future that is well within their grasp! You wrote it on an index card that, hopefully, you'll find on your mirror. Did you memorize your elevator pitch?

Say—or read—your elevator pitch out loud.

Let's say you're in an elevator right now and someone with the ability to help you steps in on floor 3 to ride with you to floor 8. If you gave your elevator pitch, would you be excited…or feel a little guilty for not quite telling the truth?

You know what to do. Thank about your elevator pitch.

Identify the real fight.
Take inventory.
Set your resolve.
Do something.

> You must always fight complacency and inflated egos.

Think back through all the topics we've discussed and all the tools you've acquired. What one or two things have you found most meaningful? Why?

I want you to go back to "Poor No More" and review Reflection Day Two—**but first, read the rest of this page for instructions.**

- Thoughtfully review what you wrote about your gifts, natural talents, and skills.

- Write any other thoughts, questions, or insights that come to mind.

- Record other examples of how you're using your gifts, talents, and skills.

By completing that Reflection Day Two, you developed an action plan. How are you doing with it? Honestly assess the steps you've taken and the progress you've made.

What rewards are you reaping from investing in yourself and your future?

Do you have a different perspective on anything you wrote previously?

Your gifts are meant to be cultivated.
Your natural talents are meant to be developed.
Your skills are meant to be sharpened.

You know what to do.

Identify the real fight.
Take inventory.
Set your resolve.
Do something.

You've got this! Until next time,
Thomas

"Life will only change when you become more committed to your dreams than you are to your comfort zone."

-BILLY COX-

Loss

When experiencing a loss, allow emotions to run their course so that success can take the baton to the finish line.

This time is important. It's time for you to think about the important people in your life. The ones who've always been there...loving you, caring for you, supporting you, and investing in your life. Their influence shapes you, and they pass their legacy on to you. Remember, don't close this book when the writing gets hard....Keep pushing. This can change your life.

> *First, change your mind. Then, change your life.*

I think the lowest point in my life so far has been the loss of my grandmother Rosa Mae Wideman. She was my rock, the central figure of my childhood.

I moved in with Grandma to look after her when I was fourteen and lived with her until I graduated from college. Living with Grandma and getting to observe her life every day was one of the greatest gifts God ever gave me.

I've been told that through my teenage years I had an unusual self-awareness and understanding about situations. It's because of Grandma. Observing the way she lived her life, the way she loved and cared for people, the way she responded to difficulty and disappointment…it all affected me deeply. Through her influence, I matured beyond my years.

Grandma's life wasn't easy. She faced challenges that could have drained the life out of anyone. But she lived with grace and strength and a resolve to make a difference in the lives of her family and friends. I tried to capture her character and the difficulty and beauty of her life in a poem I wrote about her. Here's an excerpt:

Who Is That Strong Woman

*Who is that strong woman
That would go to the ends of the Earth for her family?
During a time where the Knight Riders in
white sheets terrorized the streets,
She would walk alone miles in the dark to work.
How could a woman be so fearless?
Who is that strong woman?*

Grandma taught me so many lessons. Much of what I've shared with you I first observed in her. This is a good place to revisit a few of the keys to life I learned from Grandma.

Write what comes to mind when you read each one. What does it mean for you right now? How are you applying it in your life? If you struggle with the concept, say so. Why do you think you do?

Treat everyone with respect and love.

When things in your life aren't going well, don't look for someone to blame. Create your own future.

Treasure your family and friends.

Never let life be just about you.

Grandma left a wonderful legacy of love and wisdom. She touched so many lives. And it strikes me as I write this…now she's touching yours.

Who in your life has always been there?

Spend a few moments thinking about that person and what they mean to you. Write about them. What words describe them? What have they taught you? What have they provided for you? What are favorite memories?

Now, think about your life and the influence you have on others. What do you hope would be written about you?

> *Grandma was always there when I was growing up... I just enjoyed being with her, enjoyed being around her.*

CAVIAR TIME

Go to your private space or find a new one. Close and lock the door. Stare at yourself in the mirror. Repeat these words:

"Why now? Why couldn't I have just one more year, month, or day? Why didn't I spend more time? Why didn't I do more?

"The times that we had were special. I will refer to those memories in my time of grief. And I understand that my grieving is a long process filled with emotions that must run their course.

"The best thing I can do is press on toward my goals, because that is what my loved one would have wanted. I will love more, smile more, and laugh more. I know that my loved one is smiling down on me from heaven. God, watch over me and my family during our time of bereavement!"

Reflection *Day One*

I'm pulling for you and cheering you on! As we approach the closing chapter of this Companion Guide, don't slow down. Stay engaged with every discussion, answer every question, and take every action step. You are equipping yourself for your future. Today, we'll talk more about success and the important people in your life.

This is how change happens!

In recent chapters, I asked you to spend time thinking deeply about your perspective on success. Flip back a few pages and review what you wrote about the person who's always been there for you.

Now review what you hope would be written about you.

Did you discover anything you'd like to add to your description of success? Any perspective you want to adjust? Write about it.

_____

_____

_____

_____

_____

_____

Your perspective on success will evolve. Your investment of time, energy, and resources will be arranged and rearranged as you move through different seasons of life. Marriage, parenting, pursuit of education, and stages of your career are examples of changing life circumstances that call for a realignment of priorities to achieve success that embraces all your life—not just part of it.

> Who is that strong woman
> Who walks gracefully and without fear?

Thinking back on our recent discussions, what must success include for you no matter what season of life you are in?

I have an overwhelming sense of gratitude when I think of Grandma and her impact on my life. For years I was gifted with her presence every single day. I live with regret that I didn't spend more time with her after I started my career and began raising my own family. I wish I had been more intentional.

I'll say again that I want you to learn from my journey, so take these words to heart:

- Cherish your loved ones.
- Tell them what they mean to you. Often.
- Be intentional. Visit them. Call them. Send them cards and pictures.
- Learn all you can about their story. Interview them, record it, write it down.
- Remember that when they're gone, you can't get them back.

Earlier in this chapter you wrote about a special person who has always been there for you. If they're still with you, tell them what you wrote. Do it in person if possible. Just let them know what they mean to you. If they've already passed, read what you wrote out loud—and pray a prayer of thanks for them. Then tell someone else what they meant to you.

Until next time,
Thomas

Reflection *Day Two*

You've invested a lot of time and energy in working through this Companion Guide, and you *will* reap rewards from doing so if you put the lessons into practice. Today, we're going to revisit critical concepts from early chapters. I've included the chapter titles so you can refer back to them, but first write as much as you can from what you've internalized.

This is how change happens!

"POOR NO MORE"

Do you think back to your "in the ditch" moment often?

When you do—or when you think back to any difficult incident in your past—does it still cause negative emotions?

What negative emotions are you currently struggling with? Finish these statements for what you are experiencing:

If I feed my _____ my _____ will grow.

If I feed my _____ my _____ will grow.

If I feed my _____ my _____ will grow.

Here are the three keys we discussed for changing your mind about your negative emotions. How are you doing with them?

- Be brutally honest.
- Examine the root.
- Tell yourself the truth.

"PEER PRESSURE AND RACE"

What is a stereotype?

What is an assumption?

Have you recently encountered someone speaking negatively about a group of people? What happened?

Did you have a response ready to push back against the negative stereotype and false assumption they were acting on? What did you say? And how did they respond?

Are you getting to know people who are different from you?

What is the most difficult part of rejecting negative stereotypes and false assumptions?

> How could her heart be filled with that much love for people? Who is that strong woman?

"THE THOMAS SPECIAL"

Are you paying attention to the messages you take in every day?

Are most of them positive messages or negative? Do they cause you to have positive or negative feelings about yourself and your life?

To what and to whom do you give most of your attention?

How many hours a week are you devoting to entertainment—movies, internet, Facebook, Instagram, etc.? What changes have you made since beginning this journey?

Have you made any intentional changes in the people you allow to influence you? If so, what changes have you made?

You've got this! Until next time,
Thomas

"I alone cannot change the world, but I can cast a stone across the waters to create many ripples."

-MOTHER TERESA-

Fine Caviar

Discover and walk in your purpose.

This time is important. It's time for you to think about your past. Because I know the future you dream of is possible, I want you to understand how important it is to look at your past. My hope is that you will begin that process now and continue it because it will empower you for your future. Remember, don't close this book when the writing gets hard.... Keep pushing. This can change your life.

> *First, change your mind. Then, change your life.*

Looking back on the past isn't easy, but examining your past helps you get clarity on your future. In his book *Emotionally Healthy Spirituality*, author Peter Scazzero describes it as "going back in order to go forward." As I worked on my book, I devoted a lot of time to examining my past. At times, I was afraid of the truth, but that's what it takes. Looking backward is important for your success, so I want to give you some keys for doing it in a healthy way.

- See your past as just that—*your past*. You cannot change it, but you can move forward and shape your future.

- Don't look for someone or something to blame. Look for reasons and seek understanding—but don't look to give yourself excuses.
- Don't be too critical of yourself. You didn't know in your past what you know now. You did the best with what you had.
- Never beat yourself up over something you did in the past. Learn from choices you regret and don't repeat the mistakes.
- Look for the positive.

Let's revisit these keys. You will need to devote significant and ongoing time to examining your past to get clarity on your future. It requires more than we can do here, but this opportunity to journal will give you a start. Reconciling with your past is critical for moving freely into your future. If you find examining your past stressful, I encourage you to seek the help of a counselor or one of your trusted few who can truly be objective.

See your past as just that—your past. **You cannot change it, but you can move forward and shape your future.** Can you acknowledge that your past is your *past*? Are you resentful about your past? Are you beginning to feel empowered to shape your future even though you cannot change your past? Why?

Don't look for someone or something to blame. Look for reasons and seek understanding—but don't look to give yourself excuses. What or who shaped your attitudes and behaviors? What or who set your expectations? What messages did you hear repeated? Was your family and home life stable?

Don't be too critical of yourself. You didn't know in your past what you know now. You did the best with what you had. Are you critical of yourself when you look back? Why is it important for you to give yourself grace?

Never beat yourself up over something you did in the past. Learn from choices you regret and don't repeat the mistakes. Are you beating yourself up over a decision or action in your past? Did you learn from it? Are you repeating the same bad choice? Are you able to let it go?

Look for the positive. Who were the people in your life who showed you love and care? Family members? Friends? Teachers? Even in hard circumstances, what positive traits did you learn?

> *"If you know better, then do better." —Grandma*

Take a few deep breaths, then spend a few minutes thinking deeply about what we've discussed.

Now, be your own compassionate friend. What do you want or need to say to yourself about your past. Go ahead—write it.

> *You can't change anything about your past, but you can change yourself and shape your future. Focus on that.*

FINAL CAVIAR TIME

Go to your private space or find a new one. Close and lock the door. Stare at yourself in the mirror. Repeat these words:

"God, thank You for everything that You have done for my loved ones and me. We are truly blessed. Thank You for my wisdom, patience, and understanding. Thank You for continuing to grow and lead me toward my purpose.

"Please continue to work through me, and all your angels on earth, to make this a better place for ALL. The world has so much potential when we put aside our differences and work together. I see it on a smaller scale when I work on expensive projects, especially those that involve teamwork across different nationalities and economic or social backgrounds.

"God, thank You for all that You've done for me!"

Reflection *Day One*

You are almost there—almost to the finish line of this Companion Guide. My hope and prayer is that you are more excited than ever about the possibilities of your future, about all you can and will achieve, and all you have to offer to the world. Today, we'll talk a bit more about examining your past to get clarity on your future.

This is how change happens!

Reflecting on my past and the stories I've shared with you allowed me to identify three things that have served as my guides. I discuss them in my book, but I mention them here because I want you to see how examining my past enabled me to understand *why* I have been guided by them.

- The invisible judge.
- My reputation.
- My competitive nature.

THE INVISIBLE JUDGE.

I've known since I was a child that because I am black not everyone can see me for who I am. I've had the sense there is an invisible judge peering over my shoulder, ever watching to see if I am being "a credit to my race." Because I've felt a responsibility to dismantle stereotypes and pave the way for other minorities, I have always given my absolute best to every endeavor and exceeded expectations.

MY REPUTATION.

In my book I share, "Growing up, I was told I would never be anything. That was a lie. So now, my reputation is everything to me." I keep my word. I go the last mile. I bust my butt to do all I can. I want people to say, "Oh, man, that Thomas guy is the real deal. He sticks to his word."

MY COMPETITIVE NATURE.

I would not be where I am without my competitive nature. My upbringing demanded it. While so much of my life's circumstances were out of my control, I *was* in control of my own effort. My competitive nature guided me through the academic success that was critical for me to rise above poverty.

Does my sharing this help you better understand the importance of examining your past to get clarity on your future? Do you see how important it is to look to the past for *reasons*—not to pass blame or find excuses?

List a few things that guide you.

_____

_____

_____

_____

_____

_____

As you think carefully about your past, can you identify *why* you are guided by these things? Where did each guide have its beginning? What influenced it?

> I am not on the highest mountain, but I climbed this one.

Above everything, the most profound driver in my life is a sense of purpose. As I share in my book:

I honestly believe that God created everyone with a purpose, and that the meaning of life is finding one's purpose and fulfilling it to your utmost.

Do you have a sense of purpose?

Write about your purpose.

I strongly recommend that you read Rick Warren's *The Purpose Driven Life*. It had a profound impact on Melanie and me. Without a sense of purpose, you will find yourself unfulfilled. It is the fuel for every goal, for every dream.

Until next time,
Thomas

Reflection *Day Two*

You've reached the final Reflection Day. You've shown yourself that you're in this for the long haul. You have a wonderful future that is worth working for. You have gifts to offer the world. You have a purpose. You are on your way! Today, we'll again visit critical concepts from earlier chapters. The chapter titles are included so you can refer back to them, but first write as much as you can from what you've internalized.

This is how change happens!

"DEATH OF A ROLE MODEL"

What is your definition of a role model? Has that definition shifted since you first wrote about it?

Who is your role model(s)?

It's been some time since we discussed being a role model. What do you most desire to learn from your role model?

Are you keeping in mind that *you* are someone's role model? What does that mean to you? Is it something that guides you in your decisions and behavior?

"I AM NEVER GETTING MARRIED"

If you are not married, what are your expectations of marriage?

If you *are* married, what *were* your expectations of marriage? Were they accurate?

Since we last discussed it, have you identified a couple you know with a happy, healthy marriage?

Who is it?

Have you talked to them to learn their story and how they maintain a healthy marriage?

> *Here I stand, ready for the next adventure.*

Is a healthy marriage a concern for you right now?

My hope is that you will be intentional about a healthy marriage, whether you're already married or hope to be. Healthy marriages don't just happen. They take work. And every moment of work is worth it.

"CONTROL YOUR RESPONSE"

What does *self-discipline* mean to you?

Write down some positive benefits that you now connect with *self-discipline*.

How are you doing with *self-discipline*?

You've got this!
Thomas

P.S. Don't forget to read my final thoughts on the next page.

"Old ways won't open new doors."

-ANONYMOUS-

Final Thoughts

*Where you start in life does not have
to be where you end up.*

You've done it! I hope and pray that completing this Companion Guide will prove to be the launching pad for your journey to a fulfilled, happy, prosperous life.

You've focused on your gifts, natural talents, and skills.

You've identified your trusted few, people you want to learn from, and someone for whom you can be a role model.

You've thought deeply about stereotypes, stress, priorities, and action steps.

You've evaluated your self-discipline and wrestled with the meaning of success.

You've looked at how you invest your time—and you've dared to start looking at your past to get clarity on your future.

And you've accomplished *so much more*.

Let this be the beginning. Keep going. Keep learning. Do the hard work.

Live your purpose to the utmost.

When I think of you…

> …I imagine your fulfillment and joy in the future you shape.
>
> …I imagine the difference you'll make by giving your gifts to the world.
>
> …I imagine what will happen because you treat everyone with love and respect.
>
> …I imagine lives being changed because you show someone else the way.

Thank you for allowing me to share the journey with you.
Thomas

PROFESSIONAL TIDBITS

from

Welfare Cheese *to* **Fine Caviar**

PROFESSIONAL TIDBIT
FROM POOR NO MORE

Regardless of their socioeconomic upbringing, some young professionals arrive at a corporation with what I call a "Welfare Cheese Mindset." This mindset consists of one or more of the following:

1. Risk averse – afraid to take calculated risks, even with management approval.

2. Zero accountability – it is always someone or something else's fault.

3. Poor work ethic – late to meetings, doesn't meet deadlines, poor quality of work, and takes shortcuts.

4. Reactive – has limited to no vision, always waits for things to happen versus making things happen, and are physically and emotionally affected by job events.

5. Nearsighted – focuses on the obstacle instead of the overall objective.

6. Self-centered – concerned with what is happening to them instead of what they can do to improve the project or team; only cares about themselves.

7. Misguided – plans to work harder after they receive the promotion instead of making themselves assets that the team cannot do without.

8. Sensitive – receives constructive feedback as an attack on their ability and reputation rather than an opportunity for continuous improvement.

9. Stereotypical – searches for or expects the bad from people versus taking time to get to know people.

10. Insecure – takes their lack of knowledge as a weakness and tries to hide it versus embracing it as an opportunity to learn and better themselves.

11. Inflated ego – focuses solely on making themselves appear great instead of promoting the accomplishments of their peers, manager, or team.

12. Hard-work-only-mentality – believes that their hard work alone will be noticed and result in a raise or promotion. *(Some self-promotion is needed when networking with professionals who can help your career.)*

13. Peer-driven – places higher value on what their friends and coworkers think of them instead of what is best for the corporation.

Don't panic if you possess one or more of these traits. We're human and a product of our upbringing, experiences, and education. The key is to recognize these traits and work to do the opposite. I have done so and have received numerous "Top Performer" or "Exceeds Expectations" ratings throughout my career. In 2010, Bill S., the Vice President of Engineering and Construction, named me one of the ten most influential people in my subsidiary's $3 billion environmental project portfolio. Being a plant engineer at the time, I felt honored to be recognized out of hundreds of employees (maybe more) who worked on the project.

The point is that corporations have invested a lot of time and money in bringing you onboard. They believe that you have potential to be a huge asset for them. They also understand that you do not know everything. They only expect that you hit the ground running by learning the business, contributing in whatever way you can, and getting to know your team and the company. Employees with a "Welfare Cheese Mindset" do not last long.

Stephen Covey's *The Seven Habits of Highly Effective People* is a must-read for any professional who is serious about career advancement. Covey's book will help you in your personal life as well. The seven habits are as follows:

1. **Be proactive.** Respond according to values, be accountable for your actions, understand and increase your circle of influence, and become a transition figure to benefit yourself and others.

2. **Begin with the end in mind.** Create and apply personal and organizational mission statements as constitutions for daily living. Envision the desired results and important values to guide activities and endeavors.

3. **Put first things first.** Focus on what's truly important (i.e., preparation, prevention, values clarification, planning, relationship-building, empowerment). Plan weekly and implement daily based on your mission, roles, goals, and priorities.

4. **Think win-win.** Balance courage and consideration in seeking mutual benefit. Ensure win-win outcomes, despite past win-lose conditioning.

5. **Seek first to understand, then to be understood.** Use empathetic listening, paying attention to another person with compassion, feeling, insight, and emotional identification.

6. **Synergize.** Explore possibilities that will benefit all involved parties.

7. **Sharpen the saw.** Renew your physical, mental, spiritual, and social/emotional lives daily. This will sustain and

increase your capacities and help discipline your mind, body, and spirit.

Purchase and read his book today. You won't regret it.

PROFESSIONAL TIDBIT
FROM PEER PRESSURE AND RACE

The kid who lunged a knife at me is no different than the coworker who tried to attack my character or quality of work, took credit for my work, or lied about me. He perceived me as a threat and chose to attack me to distinguish himself in some way. The mechanic who said that I received my job because I was black is another example. He thought that I would respond with anger or be discouraged. The plant manager who told me I was doing a great job each time I met with him, but told other plant managers that I was not leadership material just before pulling me out of the leadership development program is another. He thought that he ended my upward mobility. I can go on and on. They formed negative opinions of me before I could speak a word, perform a task, or deliver a result.

But I smiled and worked harder and smarter. Before I knew it, I was delivering results on some of the most challenging capital-intensive projects. I had something to prove to myself, not to them. In all these cases, each became a close ally or supporter. As Grandma would say, "Kill them with kindness."

The few times that I responded to those attacks with a little emotion, like frowning or simply ignoring them, I was deemed as the angry black male. This affected my professional advancement. I would receive bonuses and raises but was never considered for management positions because of "something that happened at so and so." The crazy thing is that no one (including me) knew what happened at so and so. This went on for years until Darryl, an angel from above, gave me an opportunity in a new role for the corporation. Having worked with Darryl (when he was a new engineer) in successfully installing, commissioning, operating, and maintaining over $1.5 billion in environmental capital projects over seven years, Darryl knew that I was the only one skilled enough to perform the job. No one else had that experience or exposure. Needless to say, I exceeded everyone's expectations.

Have you ever watched *The Tudors, Versailles, Rome,* or any other medieval movie or television series? Pay close attention to the interactions between the nobles in the court. They attack each other with grace and a smile. A perceived threat to one's honor could lead to death or imprisonment. Therefore, they avoid it unless they want war.

Never respond with anger or too much excitement. If a person upsets you, simply smile, accept the criticism, and walk away. If the attacks persist, discuss the problem with your manager then privately plan how you can turn it into an advantage or simply plan your exit especially if your manager doesn't address it. Outthink your opponents. Always deliver more than expected and treat people like you want to be treated, even if you feel they do not deserve it. No one can take away your performance or your personality. Take the higher ground.

Check out Richard Carlson's *Don't Sweat the Small Stuff.* Richard discusses how often people let little things get them all worked up. Upon closer examination, however, those little things aren't really that big of a deal. He provides nearly one hundred ideas that you can practice to become kinder, wiser, happier, more patient, and less stressed. Other helpful books are Robert Greene's *The 48 Laws of Power* and Sun Tzu's *The Art of War.* Both books are must-reads for the young upward-bound professional. They each use history to discuss the time-tested strategies that people employ to obtain power.

PROFESSIONAL TIDBIT FROM THE THOMAS SPECIAL

Early in my career, I attended a multi-day leadership conference. During the day, we would attend seminars and workshops. In the evenings, we would participate in fun social events that contained a large variety of food and alcohol. This was both entertaining and educational. I would watch some low-level entry supervisors get sloppy drunk and have to be escorted to their rooms.

It was a different story for the executives and rising stars, though. They would drink a little as they worked the room, getting to know everyone. They always remained in control. It turns out that some were working on their next promotion. Sure enough, the announcement would arrive weeks later.

If you work for a company long enough, you will be invited to after-work social events. Never overindulge, because you are always being watched and judged. Some of your peers are measuring their competition while managers are assessing how you would interact with important clients or executives.

Do you know how you should dress for these events? Should you wear a black tie to a black-tie event? (*I did on stage in front of hundreds of small business owners and government officials at a major business conference in Washington DC, sponsored by the U.S. Department of Commerce. Yikes!*) Do you know which silverware you should use for multi-course meals? (*Hint: work from the outside in.*)

Letitia Baldridge's *New Complete Guide to Executive Manners* can help you. From eating with chopsticks to running meetings to entertaining clients, Letitia doesn't miss anything. She will show you how to perform flawlessly in every business situation.

PROFESSIONAL TIDBIT FROM THE DEATH OF A ROLE MODEL

When I first joined the leadership development program as a young engineer, I met Allen, a young mechanical engineer from Tuskegee University. Allen was a cool brother who would give you the clothes off his back. Although he worked at a plant that was more than twenty miles away, we kept in touch.

Shortly after our corporation was sued for racial discrimination by a handful of former employees, all employees were required to attend diversity training. Allen and I attended one of the first classes. This was one of the most uncomfortable classes. There were twenty or more people in the room and only three black people and even fewer women and other minorities. The subject was about how diversity was a strength, or how they should treat me (or so I thought).

During one exercise, the instructor posted blank sheets around the room. Each sheet covered a demographic (i.e., black, white, gay, women, Baptist, Muslim, Hispanic). Each attendee had to write a misconception that they had heard about each demographic on a Post-it Note, then stick it on the respective sheet. Next, the instructor asked for volunteers to read each sheet.

Allen volunteered to read the one about black people. He had a huge grin as he exited our table, but that quickly changed after he started to read some of the Post-it Notes. Some of the offensive ones included lazy, dumb, and chicken eaters. Tears formed in his eyes.

After reading a few of the notes aloud, Allen turned to his classmates and yelled, "If you all think this about me, then f— all of you." The room went quiet for a few minutes before the instructor cleverly described Allen's frustration as one that all minorities have lived with their entire lives.

I would like to believe that the exercise exacerbated Allen's "Welfare Cheese Mindset," affecting his work relationships and performance. About a year later, my engineering manager requested that I help Allen. He said that Allen was not performing well at his plant. So I did. I talked to him to learn about what was troubling him, shared my experiences and how I overcame them, and offered to help in any way (including helping with his job tasks). He declined my assistance, saying that he had everything under control. A few years later, he was fired for low performance ratings.

I follow Allen on LinkedIn and noticed that he has moved from company to company over the last thirteen years and has not stayed longer than three years at any one company. I attribute some of my later career hurdles to Allen's old plant manager viewing me as Allen.

In Les Brown's *It's Not Over Until You Win*, Les talks about eliminating toxic and energy-draining people from your life in lesson seven. He explains how toxic people are not out to intentionally destroy you; it is simply that the mess they have allowed in their lives will weigh you down. Last, Les states that you can't help or change others until they choose to help or change themselves.

PROFESSIONAL TIDBIT
FROM I AM NEVER GETTING MARRIED

Do you think you can keep your personal life separate from your professional life? Think again. You spend most of your awake hours at work, approximately 45 percent of a seven-day week. This number approaches 50 percent, depending on your commute and the amount of business travel. That is a long time to hide emotions that may have originated at home. Just ask Ryan.

Ryan graduated from Georgia Tech with a mechanical engineering degree. Not only was he extremely smart, but he was also personable and empathetic. Everyone—managers, secretaries, and janitors included—liked Ryan. He was a rising star.

At that time, Ryan was dating his college sweetheart, who had to have been a cheerleader. By the time she became his fiancée, she'd become an attorney at a big law firm and was already starting to make a name for herself. Their wedding was extravagant, not a detail missed. They both seemed so happy. Then they purchased a new home and cars.

Ryan had everything going well for him: a beautiful wife with a promising career, an upward path to executive management, and an expensive home in a premier school district. Everyone, including me, wanted to be like Ryan: living a Ken-and-Barbie, Beverly Hills lifestyle, without having to work twice as hard for it. (But there are some things I can't change about myself.)

After the couple had their first child, things changed. Ryan's wife quit her job to stay home and raise the baby. Being old-fashioned, Ryan supported that move. Over the next year, Ryan's demeanor began to change. Normally at ease in all situations, including crises, Ryan reacted negatively to everything.

Caring about my friend, I invited him to lunch. Ryan was under a lot of financial stress. In addition to the mortgage and auto loans, he financed a large fraction of the wedding costs including the honeymoon using his credit cards. It turns out that Ryan wasn't the rich white kid I had envisioned.

"Chill," I said empathetically. "The best way to get out of this hole is to stop digging."

"But my wife has expensive tastes," he replied helplessly.

"Well, you have to make a choice," I said as if I were his father. "If you continue on your current path, you will not have a job because no one will want to work with you."

I pulled out a napkin and had the waitress bring me a pen. I did what all chemical engineers do when performing material and energy balances. I drew a box. First, we constructed the arrows leaving the box (i.e., loan payments, cost of living expenses like utilities, car maintenance, taxes, and other cash outflows). Second, I listed what was in the box like savings, checking, investments accounts, cash under the mattress, etc. Third, we drew the arrows entering the box. For him, the only cash inflow was his salary each month. Finally, I asked him to take the napkin home and fill in the blanks. Using a simple formula (total inflows subtract total outflows), I asked "Is the box shrinking?" In other words, are you spending more than you're earning? I didn't want to know his salary, because it would probably have upset me.

The next day, he arrived at work a new man. His box was shrinking but was recoverable with a few lifestyle changes. Now the hard work began: convincing his wife. They took my advice and met with a financial planner. Over the next few weeks, they had some tough discussions, but their love conquered all in the end.

My pastor, Bishop Dale C Bronner, once said, "Women enter marriages thinking they can change their husbands, while men enter marriages expecting that their wives will not change." Both are flawed expectations. Before you decide to get married, check out Marlo Thomas's and Phil Donahue's *What Makes a Marriage Last* and Gary Chapman's *The 5 Love Languages: The Secret to Love That Lasts*. You can have a long, successful marriage if both of you are aligned and commit to working on the marriage throughout.

PROFESSIONAL TIDBIT
FROM CONTROL YOUR RESPONSE

Chiquita was a talented electrical engineer from the University of Florida. But, man, was she overly sensitive. Any little thing could set her off.

One morning, our manager didn't respond to Chiquita's greeting. She repeated herself louder, almost yelling, then the manager responded.

"I think he is prejudiced," she said after the manager walked away.

"No, he is just a butthole to everyone—white, black, family, etc." I responded, referring to past observations of him in meetings and at annual family picnics at the plant.

"I hear you, but I think the man has a problem with black people, especially black women," she snarled.

The manager treated everyone that way. There were numerous times that I would greet him with "Good morning, Rich" only to receive no response, sometimes not even a smile. But that didn't bother me. In fact, Rich was a very intelligent and resourceful engineer who rewarded his people handsomely for delivering positive results. He just had terrible interpersonal skills.

At the end of the year, Rich met with us individually to discuss our performance. I received a rating of "Above Expectations" and Chiquita received "Meets Expectations." She was livid. She went to her cubicle for thirty minutes then visited mine and grabbed me by the arm, taking me to a private room so that we could talk.

"He had the nerve to say that I needed to improve the quality of my work, arrive to meetings on time, and not spend so much on meals during business travel!" she screamed.

"Calm down, Chiquita," I replied. "On the surface it sounds bad, but you received a 'Meets.' You can bounce back from this."

"I'm going to report him to Ethics," she said as if a light bulb had turned on in her head.

"Be careful," I cautioned her. "On what cause?"

She didn't respond. Later, she came to her senses and decided not to file a complaint. She never fully recovered, however. A few months later, she left the company and moved back home to Florida.

Chiquita could have easily become a manager in our company once she cleaned up a few bad habits. In fact, our manager mentioned that during her performance review. She was one of a few women engineers in the company. At that time, there was a push to coach, train, and mentor women engineers into leadership roles.

In Napoleon Hill's *Think and Grow Rich*, Napoleon talks about how you cannot achieve anything if you do not take control of your thoughts and actions. He states that we are creatures of habit, but, because we are a mind with a body, we can change our habits. "If you do not conquer self, you will be conquered by self" is one of my favorite quotes in the book.

Think first and act afterwards. Shape the patterns of your thoughts to harmonize with your goals and purposes. Keep your mind busy with a definite purpose backed by a definite plan of action. And you will soon discover that unexpected events, including crises, do not affect you as much as they affect everyone else.

PROFESSIONAL TIDBIT FROM THE PAYOFF

Time and time again, I have witnessed young professionals, shortly after graduating and getting that first job, buy a new truck, car, boat, or home. When I ask them why, they respond that they deserve it and can afford the payments (with no mention of the principal, term, or interest).

Do you remember Ryan's story from earlier? Hypothetically, let's consider his payment obligations after his wife quit her job:

Ryan's Salary = $7,083/month ($85,000)

Item	Monthly Payment
Car loan payment (two new cars)	$750 (total)
Home mortgage	$1,100
Credit card debt for wedding (min payment)	$100
Benefits, 401(k), and taxes (federal, state, property, etc.)	$2,433
Food (add more for full family)	$600
Home maintenance (i.e., yard, repairs)	$200
Car maintenance (i.e. fuel, oil changes, tires, repairs)	$592
Bills and utilities	$707
Health and fitness	$50
Church and charities	$100
Shopping	$100
Insurances (life, auto, liability, etc.)	$240
Net income (leftover money)	**$111**

Suppose that Ryan purchased mediocre cars and donated one percent to church and charity. Ryan and his wife would have $111 remaining each month. This had to be a shock to their lifestyle after removing his wife's nearly $100,000 salary.

Now let's analyze this another way:

Item	Commitment
Two new cars (cars last 7-10 years)	5 years per car
Home mortgage	15–30 years
Credit card debt for wedding (minimum payment)	30 years or more
Benefits, 401K, and taxes (federal, state, property, etc.)	Permanent
Food	Grows with family
Home maintenance (i.e., yard, repairs)	Permanent
Car maintenance (i.e. oil changes, tires, repairs)	Permanent
Bills and utilities	Permanent
Health and fitness	Permanent
Church and charities	Permanent
Shopping	Permanent
Insurances (auto, home, liability, etc.)	Permanent

What if Ryan did not like his job? Can he take a few months off to find a new one? What if he receives a crazy assignment? Can he refuse it, knowing that it may stifle future growth and promotion?

Eric Tyson's *Personal Finance for Dummies* and *Investing for Dummies* are great books about maintaining and growing your personal wealth. Eric explains how everyone should use software like Quicken and Mint to track their finances weekly and develop a budget. He also explains that you should make your investments automatic so that you can save for retirement, plan for a big purchase, or add another income stream.

Wealth is more than money. It is having the freedom to make choices that you want to make versus those that you must make. Wealth is also time, a commodity you cannot get back.

One of my fellow chemical engineering graduates has not worked for anyone for more than fifteen years. The book that I will introduce in the next professional tidbit changed his and his wife's (also a chemical engineer) lives forever. They are one of the couples we vacation with every year.

PROFESSIONAL TIDBIT
FROM LIFE IS SHORT, LIVE IT WELL

Whether you love your job or not, you should always prepare for an emergency or life-changing event. Taking this one step further, you should plan for a future layoff, manager change, or pay reduction. Since you are living opposite of the "Welfare Cheese Mindset," those seem like unlikely events. However, study the financial crisis of 2007 or 2008, the COVID-19 pandemic of 2020, or the Great Depression during the 1930s.

Don't rush to build a bunker in your backyard and stack it with canned goods. Instead, read books about personal finance, investing, and business. Establish an emergency fund with at least 6 months of expenses. Slowly develop other income streams (arrows flowing into your box).

In the last chapter, I introduced a couple that I admire quite a bit. Their names are Rodney and Kellee. We were in the same chemical engineering graduating class. Kellee was extremely smart, a 4.0 GPA chemical engineering student. Rodney was smart as well. Upon graduating, they both went to work for ExxonMobil in Houston, Texas.

In 2002, Kellee and Rodney, Eulah and Mike (also graduates of the University of South Carolina), and my wife and I and took our first vacation together in Jamaica. Not only did we have fun exploring the resort, participating in excursions, and relaxing by the pool and beach, we discussed family, career, and future. We had such a great time that we have vacationed together every year since.

During one of those early vacations, I introduced Robert Kiyosaki's *Rich Dad Poor Dad: What the Rich Teach Their Kids about Money That the Poor and Middle Class Do Not!* That book changed our lives. We all started buying rental properties. While I have since exited that space, the remaining two couples are still investing. But Kellee and Rodney took it to another level, allowing Rodney to leave his job after a few years, pay off the debt on their rental properties, and travel around the world.

From time to time, I would find similar books, like Lee Jenkins' *Taking Care of Business: Establishing a Financial Legacy for the African American Family*, and share them with my friends. Lee's book moved me so much that I purchased ten copies and shipped them to my closest friends. Rodney introduced George Clason's *The Richest Man in Babylon* to us.

Earn a great living while on the job but build wealth in your spare time.

PROFESSIONAL TIDBIT
FROM SHARPEN YOUR FOCUS

Career setbacks can come unexpectedly. You can be passed over for a promotion, receive a different manager, or be affected by changing business conditions. And this can happen when you are performing at the top of your game, exceeding everyone's expectations. I have had my share of setbacks. Some of them were caused by my "Welfare Cheese Mindset." Here are a few:

1. **Networking** - Being an introvert early in my career, I focused on my performance. And I was good. One of my Leadership Development peers told me that I should schedule meetings with upper managers and express my interest in management positions. I smiled but chose to focus on delivering superior results instead. Result: he is a politically savvy vice president and I am a talented program manager.

2. **Manager Change** - I was performing at a high level in a position that the company had created for me. I was untouchable, or so I thought. Then my manager received a promotion. The next manager was good but was soon replaced by a young manager who had failed in a previous department management role. Friends who had worked for this person told me that I should find another job. But I felt that my superior performance and unmatched client support could overcome anything. Result: the manager was one of the worst ones I have ever had. Thankfully, I moved on to a better job in a different subsidiary. Ironically, the manager was promoted.

3. **Sensitive** - After being removed from the Leadership Development program, I decided that upper management was not for me. I chose to focus on delivering results and helping my peers achieve their career aspirations. My

friend (who was also a plant manager) told me that I should meet with my old plant manager, apologize for any misconceptions, and seek constructive feedback. Ignoring his advice, because I felt I had not done anything wrong, my career was stagnant for a few years. I constantly interviewed but never successfully landed the job. Finally, I scheduled a lunch meeting with that plant manager. To my surprise, he sang my praises and offered his support. Result: soon after, I was back on track, receiving a management promotion.

You must always fight complacency and inflated egos. You also need to understand your worth and consistently work on your career. During my recent setback, I read Dr. Karen Gurney's *Stacked: Double Your Job Interviews, Leverage Recruiters, Unlock LinkedIn*1 based on a recommendation from one of my best friends, Ernie. That recommendation was a godsend. I enjoyed Dr. Gurney's book so much that I hired her to help me find another job. She helped me assess my career worth, she revised my résumé and LinkedIn profile, and she applied for jobs on my behalf and helped me prepare for the interviews. As a result, I received two job offers (one internal and one external) in a matter of weeks. The job that I accepted was my dream job. Karen has also helped two of my friends find great jobs.

When you face adversity on your job, first evaluate yourself. Do not beat yourself down and devalue your capabilities, however. Are you meeting the expectations set at the beginning of the year? If you are, then work with someone like Karen to help you assess your value. Karen was expensive, but my friends and I agree that it was one of the greatest investments in our career.

Every great change in my life was preceded by a low point.

---

1 https://hire-a-headhunter.com. https://karengurney.com

PROFESSIONAL TIDBIT
FROM LOSS

Although we want our loved ones to live happily forever, one or more of them may die unexpectedly. It can be the result of a car accident, bad health, a pandemic, suicide, a crime, or simply old age. Even if we anticipate it, we cannot predict how we will respond.

During my grandma's last days in the hospital, I observed that grief affects people differently. Some relatives were sad that this matriarch who held this family together for decades was finally meeting her end. They could not let her go and insisted that the family invest whatever costs to keep Grandma alive on a machine. Others had feelings of regret. They felt that they could have visited Grandma more and possibly helped prolong her life. Some relatives were angry. Rather than deal with their emotions, they got wasted and wanted to fight other relatives. A handful of us kept a level head, at least when others were around.

When it was just me and Grandma, I wept like a baby. During those periods of weakness, I emailed some friends, including some coworkers. Most of them were true friends who cared for me and offered their sympathy and support. One of them told others that I was a drama queen. *Really?*

The loss of a loved one is life's most stressful event and can cause a major emotional crisis. You may not be prepared for the intensity and duration of your emotions or how swiftly your moods may change. You may even begin to doubt the stability of your mental health. But be assured that these feelings are healthy and appropriate and will help you come to terms with your loss. It takes time to fully absorb the impact of a major loss. You never stop missing your loved one, but the pain eases after time and allows you to go on with your life.

Be careful with what you share with your coworkers, especially during periods of weakness.

The Mental Health America1 website offers advice on how to help others deal with loss. They are as follows:

1. Allow them to share their feelings. This is therapeutic and helps them make sense of their emotions.
2. Don't offer false support by saying "it was for the best." How do you know? Are you God?
3. Offer practical help. Volunteer to babysit or perform their work tasks or other errands to save them time.
4. Be patient. It will take them time to work through their feelings.
5. Encourage professional help when necessary. Our corporation offers services to help employees deal with loss, divorce, and other events that occur in their personal lives.
6. Bonus: regardless of how they act, treat them with as much love and compassion as you can.

---

1 Mental Health America, "Bereavement and Grief," Bereavement and Grief, accessed January 28, 2021, https://www.mhanational.org/bereavement-and-grief.

PROFESSIONAL TIDBIT FROM FINAL THOUGHTS

Why am I on earth? Without government assistance, my mom could not afford to feed and clothe me. When I was a teen and contemplating suicide, why didn't God allow me to carry it out? I could not provide any value to anyone. When it appeared that society had turned its back on us, how did I survive when some of my friends didn't? My friends and I were thugs. What can I offer people? I am not a celebrity, executive, or rich.

Many people believe that their purposes arise from their special gifts and sets them apart from other people. That is only part of the truth. It also grows from their connection to others. Once they find their paths and help others achieve their dreams, they will achieve greatness.

Rick Warren's *The Purpose-Driven Life* sends the reader on a forty-day spiritual adventure to find one's purpose. In addition to reading the book, my wife and I participated in a multi-week *Purpose-Driven Life* workshop via our church. It was enlightening. We met some lifelong friends and I credit the book and workshop with helping Mel and I refine our purpose.

What is my purpose?

1. To constantly push myself, my family, and everyone around me toward greatness. Every obstacle overcome is a sign that God is in our corner.

2. To build up and celebrate people around me. Every person has a God-given gift.

3. To be a testimony to others that they can overcome anything with focus, patience, determination, and faith.

God puts us through different experiences to strengthen and build us for something great that is coming next.

4. To tear down as many false stereotypes as possible. We can help God show people his greatness by giving others a chance to better themselves.

5. To build generational wealth (i.e., assets, income, knowledge, relationships, love). God want us to grow his kingdom.

When you discover your purpose, you will walk around with a joy that few can take from you. You will have a wider view of life's events. Things will appear to be easy to you. You will continue to have challenges. But your perception of them will be different.

About the Author

Thomas Wideman was born and raised in the grip of poverty, forced to mature fast. In those critical moments, he decided to transcend his circumstances through academic achievement. Student body vice president and starting cornerback on the varsity football team, these ventures served as positive distractions from at-home struggles and leverage on college applications.

After high school, he joined the U.S. Army Reserve as a Chemical Operations Specialist. Afterwards, he graduated from the University of South Carolina with a BS in Chemical Engineering and from Georgia State University with an MBA in Finance.

His memoir, *Welfare Cheese to Fine Caviar*, shares his most transformative life experiences to help fulfill his mission of improving society one person at a time. When he isn't working, Thomas enjoys spending quality time with his wife, Melanie, a civil engineer and owner of A Little Slice of Heaven Bakery, and their sons, Isaiah and Noah.

We believe that the majority of us love our fellow human being regardless of race, gender, religion, sexual preference, or other demographic. We must resist racism and extremism at all costs.

Let's set people up for success by:

1. Providing them the opportunities and tools to achieve their goals

2. Helping and encouraging them to learn from their failures.

3. Celebrating their accomplishments.

Regardless of our political affiliations, let's all work on bringing our country back to the center where healthy debate and compromise leads to prosperous lives for everyone.

Currently, we are a small organization that sells motivational products (books, posters, shirts, etc.). However, our goal is to help the less fortunate pave successful paths in the world.

www.ingramcontent.com/pod-product-compliance
Lightning Source LLC
Chambersburg PA
CBHW072151100526
44589CB00015B/2180